THE CHRONICLES OF LARRY, VOLUMES ONE AND TWO.

John Archer-Thomson

First published in Great Britain 2008 by John Archer-Thomson

Copyright© John Archer-Thomson 2008

ISBN: 978-0-9558572-0-1

PART, THE FIRST: Larry and His Pals.

PART, THE SECOND: Larry goes on Holiday by mistake.

The Chronicles of Larry.

Volume one: Larry and his pals.

1. Introducing Larry.

Hello there.

My name is Larry and in all honesty I am a limpet. There it is out in the open from the outset like the pride and joy of an over-enthusiastic flasher. I can lay no claims to greatness: Leonardo da Vinci did not develop a mysterious code to protect my identity; I am not a direct descendent of Mary Magdalene and I didn't even prove Fermat's last theorem before that British bloke beat me to it in1994.

Bugger.

It depresses me slightly (ok, a lot) that having got my identity out in the public domain most of you still won't know what the hell I'm talking about. 'Oh of course, one of those' is not the anticipated reaction and you may well have that puzzled expression on your face like when you found you had won a particle accelerator at Bingo.

Never mind, I'm here to enlighten you. Nobody will doubt your grasp on life's essentials again if you read this little missive. No more walks of shame from the Mastermind chair, no more little notes left on your Fridge saying 'Thicky'.

First, a bit about where we live: it's called the rocky shore. It's the bit by the sea, between high and low water mark, where nobody would think of sunbathing unless an accurate, massive budget, re-enactment of 'Kill Bill' was taking place on the sand. I suppose that is where the confusion starts, because we live on the rocks and don't move about much we often get mistaken for part of the scenery. The fact that we can move thrills some people to a state of mild hysterics but there is more to the magic world of limpets than a bit of sliding about. Read on, you will be thrilled (or not).

As appearances go (and they do) I suppose we look like the aftermath of a troupe of leprous garden gnomes going over the rocks, leaving their kneecaps behind. Yes that's about it, like little kneecaps stuck to the rocks.

Depressing really.

Now for a bit of limpet history. I don't remember my early times too well so I had a chat with some of the elders and they told me how it went, more or less. Apparently in the autumn, when the sea gets colder and rougher, limpets of male and female persuasion get into a bit of a frenzy and chuck all sorts of reproductive stuff into the sea. This stuff is extremely cunning and it knows exactly what to do. As soon as it gets the green light it zaps about in the ocean, does something a bit weird and produces a young limpet.

But this young limpet is not like the aftermath-of-the-garden-gnomes version. At this point we don't have shells, we are tiny [an extremely small, sharp-eyed person with a magnifying glass could walk past a million of us and when questioned closely about it later would say 'Limpets, what limpets?'] and we swim about in the sea for a living.

There's an awful lot of other stuff in the sea as well. I'm not sure how it all gets there but it is there and you can't argue with that. Of course you can argue with it if you want but shouting at plankton, minerals and organic detritus doesn't get you very far: it does get you some very strange looks though.

So anyway there I am drifting about, having fun in a larval sort of way, eating plants that are even smaller than I am. These little plants are also drifting about and it's their home that we are drifting about in. You might think it a touch rude to eat little plants when they are 'at home'; it's rather like being invited for tea with the Ramsgate family and devouring their offspring (Jimmy and Mabel) before the angel cakes arrive. Putting your behaviour down to extreme peckishness doesn't seem to cut the mustard with the Ramsgate progenitors so you eat them too before things get really ugly. Anyway young limpets do that sort of thing; it's part of our design.

We have a pretty fun time for about two weeks in a peripatetic sort of way but then it's time to get down to the serious business of growing a shell: this changes your life.

Imagine you are in Tesco's for the 'big shop'; all goes swimmingly until you get to the checkout. Suddenly, as you produce your credit card, you grow a shell. The cashier [up until that moment a model of friendly professionalism] suddenly gets a little frosty and rings for assistance. The manager appears, sees a customer with two hundred pounds worth of goods and Ben Nevis stuck to their back, and calls the police. Probably the best course of action is to abandon the provisions, run to the SUV, shove the shell in the back (squashing the poodle) and go home for a nice cup of tea and a massive nervous breakdown.

Well it's not like that for limpets; we are pretty casual about shell growing. Rather than Breakdown-City, Arizona it's more like Chill-out County, Wyoming.

Now just before I tell you what we do with our shell I forgot to mention one fairly major problem that has to be avoided if one is to remain with the 'in-crowd' in Drift City. There are some malicious gits about that seem determined to do a Mr & Mrs Ramsgate's revenge on young limpets. Some fish are guilty of this hideous sin and there are some even more frightening things around that would like to put young limpets through something resembling a car press. Apparently these sadists are called whales and they are not fish: well they look suspiciously like it to me. To be honest if something is about to kill you getting the taxonomic minutiae sorted out is of secondary importance I would have thought. Still it's ok because something else seems to be trying to kill all the whales (I've heard rumours of 'scientific reasons' or some such bollocks) so we won't need to worry for much longer, thank the pyramids.

So if you avoid getting eaten it's time to do something pretty important with the shell, but first an explanatory note about the colloquialism 'thank the pyramids' that the razor sharp amongst you may have noticed rearing its mysterious head in recent prose. A long time ago, before crevice became a dirty word, the Egyptians worshipped limpets. They built three very large limpets near a village called Cairo, which they revered, and even built some small ones nearby to make the big limpets think that they had had babies. Thus the big pyramidal molluscan entities would be happy and hence not blat the Egyptian's crops with massive thunderbolts. So the 'thank the pyramids' exclamation was a reference to happier times when human beings had got their act together a bit better with respect to rocky shore denizens.

Just in case you are getting a bit fed up with not knowing about the shell I'll pull a tentacle out and get on with the plot. As it would have done in Tesco's growing a shell changes the way you look at life. Suddenly you get fed up with drifting about, attending one boring plankton party after another, it all seems so meaningless and empty. What really starts to appeal is a nice little home and perhaps even a pension scheme so the next time the water currents allow you blunder onto some nearby rocks and take up residence.

Now if being small and insignificant was advantageous when you were a drifter it is a bit of a drawback when on the rocks.

I don't know if you have ever attended a jumble sale. You turn up before the doors open and there is a collection of refined, sweet-mannered, sophisticated ladies in their two-pieces all chatting away about the vicar's triumph on the croquet lawn the previous weekend. As you contemplate how spiffing it is to be wedged in amongst the vertebrae of England's very backbone the doors open.

Carnage is not too strong a word.

Suddenly limbs start flying, teeth are bared and England's vertebrae make 'The Chainsaw Massacre' look like a Sunday outing for jellyfish. If you are small and not equipped with a thermonuclear device you are likely to be disembowelled before you even get to the home made jam counter. This is what it is like to land on the bottom of the rocky shore if you are small and defenceless: completely terrifying.

Even the plants are deadly, it's like somebody has invented rubber trees (as opposed to trees that produce rubber which have been invented). At the drop of a hat they bend down and thrash you off the rocks. All very well if you are in to a bit of spanking but decidedly unhelpful for a young limpet trying to make its way in a hostile world.

You might wonder why this gormless young artefact doesn't go and get help from other limpets.

A fair question.

Well, construct if you will, dear reader, the following conceptual effigy [sorry about that I seem to have succumbed to an attack of Victorianism]. You are sightseeing in Manhattan, the day is fine and New York doesn't seem to be living up to its dangerous reputation [the recent mugging you witnessed was quite understandable as the victim had a Yorkshire terrier with a ribbon and was wearing far too much make-up: in short they were asking for it]. All of a sudden the skyscrapers start walking about (they have been feeling a little restless recently). Well getting trampled under foot by a skyscraper is about the same as being crushed by an older limpet; basically it is welcome to Pancake City either way.

So to summarise, you can get eviscerated, trampled to death or thrashed into a frenzy if you are not very careful. The only advantage of being small, less than a millimetre in fact, is that you can hide and eat until you get over the shock of it all and are big enough to fight your own battles.

Feeding on the shore is an interesting experience. Young limpets are still very much into vegetarian fare but now the food is all over the floor. The accepted procedure is to walk about the place with your tongue dragging over the ground, waving from side to side, until repleteness is achieved.

Not all young limpets land on the bottom of the shore. If you happen to be house hunting when the tide is high you may well find your dream house somewhere near the top but from what a handful of survivors have said it's not a bundle of laughs up there either. It is a bit like parachuting into the Gobi desert; if you happen to land near an oasis [for oasis read crevice or rock pool] you are laughing all the way to the sand-in-the-crevice-removal facility but if you miss the oasis it's absolutely no compensation knowing you are not going to get eaten, trampled to death or flagellated into a froth, as you die of thirst, heat stroke or even frost bite if the climate is playing silly-buggers.

Basically to survive on a rocky shore you have to be rugged: the sort of person that drinks whisky out of a dirty glass whilst biting the heads off young goats: that sort of thing. No flower arrangers allowed.

Now I suppose you are settling back and thinking, 'That's about it for limpets then, time to go and Hoover the parrot.' Well that's not quite the case, in fact there is a lot more stuff to come and some of it gets a bit smutty.

Life at the bottom of the shore ticked away like a ticky-tocky thing but there was a problem on the horizon. I'd got this place of my own on the rocks and I'd go off, drag the old tongue over the floor for a bit and then return home wondering about things like whether bananas get upset when they go squelchy. At home the time spent between feeding sessions was spent growing some more shell, respiring a bit and trying to do aerobics workouts without laughing. All around this home by the sea there were hundreds of sessile beings called barnacles, they were there when I arrived and didn't seem to mind the extra neighbour at all. But I was definitely getting bigger and even the barnacles were expanding in a couch-potato-like way.

One day the unthinkable happened.

I'd gone off for a damn good gorge and was musing over the fact that limpets are supposed to be stupid, no famous molluscan physicists for example, [there again the news is not all bad, you'll never see a limpet watching reality TV or buying a copy of the Sun] when it struck me that we know a few things that you don't.

I've heard that there are people who devote years of their life to studying limpets [so far so good]. They take them off the rocks [this is where things start to go down hill], rip them to pieces [enough already] and look at their bits under a microscope [surely that's illegal]. Why do they do all this? Apparently it is to discover how old we are and they still can't do it. Well actually it is none of their business.

Another thing that is unknown is how we find our way home. Limpets usually have a little spot on the rocks that they return to when they have finished going about their gastropodian business. It is called a 'home scar' and how we get back to it is the big mystery.

Experiments involving silly tricks like ripping defenceless limpets off the rocks and setting them down, miles away from home, are tried to see if they can return. If they can't then the limpet is deemed to be a disgrace to its family and is sent away to a correction facility. What the scientists don't know is that the limpet in question may have had a late night (out at the soup kitchen, feeding the poor) and was too shagged out to bother playing games. How would you like it if half way through a riveting DVD some bastard in a white coat broke into your living room and whisked you away to Outer Mongolia with instructions to find your way home without a GPS or map? I'm sure you would be chuffed to bits and play right along. Well anyway as to how we find our way home? Ask an Egyptian.

Sorry, I've digressed in rather a massive way there, back to the plot.

I was heading for home, mulling all this over, but when I arrived chez-moi, something was horribly wrong. I couldn't quite settle down properly and there was a nasty draft blowing in under the jolly old shell margin. I suspected foul play at first; some of the young barnacles were looking a mite too smug for my liking, but what could I do? It seemed I had grown too big for my home scar. I thought for a while and decided that there was nothing for it but to move house. [Strictly speaking that should be move home as my house (shell) is attached and I move it quite a lot, especially in the nightclubs baby]. So I girded up the old loin and headed further up the shore to what appeared to be a promising vacant lot.

All was well until something resembling Everest trundled up and promptly settled down on top of me. At first I wondered if Everest's intentions were strictly honourable but soon remembered (with a certain amount of relief) that limpets don't do that sort of thing. The minutes passed and nothing much seemed to happen (I tried to amuse myself by pretending I was experiencing a fleshy eclipse) then boredom approached like you'd expect it to, shuffling along slowly in dusty grey rags with a stick, a long beard and an expression that would frighten a grapefruit.

Suddenly Everest retreated, probably trying to remember when she had taken a calcium carbonate suppository, so I took the opportunity to beat a hasty retreat up the rocks. Eventually I found a nice, unoccupied spot that fitted my shell beautifully and was quite near a rock pool in case of emergencies. Here I decided to stay and toyed with the idea of growing a beard, big enough to hide a badger in, and a lot bigger than boredom's. Triumphant, hirsute daydreams flowed through my non-existent brain until I remembered that molluscs don't fare very well in beard growing competitions as they lack follicular capability.

Well that just about wraps up the Introduction to Larry bit. Life trundled on in a basement of the British Museum sort of way and I assumed it would continue to do so until death approached, dressed rather similarly to boredom.

How wrong I was but more of that later.

Now there is one bit about limpets that I have avoided so far, the proverbial beans have not been spilt and the jolly old cat is still in the bag and in danger of asphyxiation. The subject I refer to of course is sex.

When we have stopped drifting about in the sea and are settled on the rocks we are busy. Busy in the sort of way you would be if you had just finished forging a million pounds worth of fivers, which you had laid out for inspection, when your partner says the community police officer is at the door and fancies a quick chat and a cup of tea. We are so busy in fact that we simply don't have time to think about sex let alone do anything that might compromise our personal hygiene status.

It matters not at this point in our young lives, as we are officially 'neuter'. This means that we are not chaps or girls; in fact we are no sex at all. You could put us in a room that was simply heaving with astonishingly attractive nubiles, who had just been hypnotised to believe that sex was good for you and made you extremely rich, and an hour later not one of them would be able to open a bank account.

This rather strange state of affairs goes on for about a year or so then suddenly we all change into chaps (two of whom are hastily despatched to search for the missing nubiles but there is no sign of them and the bloke that organised the event, payment in advance, has mysteriously disappeared).

As you can imagine with lots of chaps around vast amounts of rugby football is played, car maintenance and metal work classes are well attended and inevitably somebody discovers girls. Word gets around and it all gets a bit rude.

Now there is still one rather disturbing detail to emerge.

You may have been wondering, if all the neuters change into chaps, where exactly do all the girls come from?

Ha, ha, where indeed?

No they do not leap out of giant cakes with there assets covered in sequins. They have not spent their formative years hiding in a secret embroidery retreat either. No the truth is horribly embarrassing. Some of the chaps, roughly a third in fact, change into girls after about five years of serious beer drinking and driving tanks. Nobody is quite sure why but it may be the result of wearing their pyjama bottoms the wrong way round when young or, and this is much more likely, others suspect that changing sex might be a side effect of too much Morris dancing.

Well with that deeply embarrassing admission out in the open I hope that even if you think we are serious perverts, and in a spirit of public mindedness have already contacted the Vice Squad, you at least won't mistake a limpet for a piece of rock again.

For those of a broad-minded disposition, a don't bat an eyelid if a giraffe goes past in a pink chiffon nightie sort of mind set, there is quite a bit more stuff.

Now you know Larry it is time to meet his pals.

2. Larry introduces some of his pals.

Rubber trees and the edible skating rink.

It's difficult to describe plants as pals really but without them I'd be as skeletal as Sidney the skinny thing after a year's trial on the 'Food is art (and not to be sullied by digestive sacrilege) diet'. Bosom buddies we are not but I will tell you about them anyway. You are probably familiar with trees and grass and all that sort of stuff, well we have those too only our versions are a little bizarre.

When the tide is in our trees are often to be found thrashing about like a whirling dervish that has just been plugged into the mains. None of the silent dignity of the English oak in a gentle summer breeze here. If you imagine the tallest human being you have ever seen, cement his (or her) feet to the floor, remove all his (or her) skeletal bits and watch what happens when he (or she) is hit by a hurricane (or hissicane, of course) which changes direction every few minutes, you'll have a pretty good idea of what our trees are like in a rough sea.

Bloody terrifying.

If you happen to be within striking distance you are doomed. Doomed as in you are mountain climbing and near the summit when your arms and legs suddenly turn to castor sugar: yes, that doomed.

Probably as a result of the disco lifestyle they lead when the tide is in our trees go completely legless when it goes out. What was active and wriggly becomes as inert and floppy as a punctured blow-up doll whose owner has just discovered real women. Seaweeds just lie about on the rocks like spinach at a funeral.

This strange Jekyll-and-Hyde behaviour is quite useful for some of my pals. Flat periwinkles, which look like miniaturised garden snails that have just escaped from a vat of custard, use the resting seaweed as a giant climbing frame and social rendezvous.

'Going down the floppy trees tonight then Shirl?'

'Not half, Daisy, I've got a hot date with that hulk from IT support.'

'Well just you watch yourself Shirl that winkle has got a reputation, he'll seduce you before you can say, "Good God, I thought you needed a licence for that "'.

Well anyway that's the trees. 'What about the edible skating rink?' I hear you cry in a state of barely controlled excitement. Well what indeed?

Most of us don't bother too much with the trees in a dietary sort of way. Being flung around at ninety miles an hour with your teeth wedged into a branch is not a top tip in the rocky shore denizen's 'Fun ways with food' handbook. No we tend to go for the slippery stuff all over the floor. Some of this stuff is like floppy grass; even if it moves around during the mealtime you get more of a friendly tickle than the sound thrashing to within an inch of certain death that you would have got from the trees.

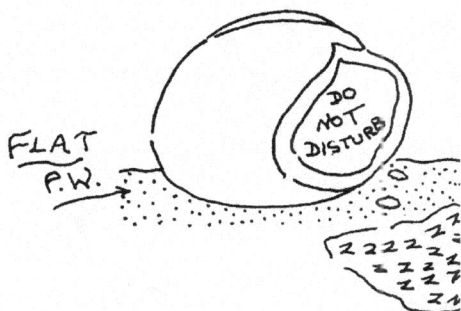

FLAT
P.W.

DO NOT DISTURB

zzzzz

Other dietary delights to be found in the Delia Smith's guide for the rocky shore gourmet include the thin layer of microscopic algae that covers the rocks. This stuff is so cunning that if you modelled a weasel out of some it would probably become Prime Minister within the week. There it is lying all innocently on the shore, whistling Ravel's Bolero quietly to itself, until a human goes anywhere near then suddenly one extremely annoyed person goes arse-over-tit and does a show-stopping impersonation of a cartilaginous waterfall. The microscopic algae, meanwhile, has stopped whistling and is quietly sniggering in an epidermal sort of way.

Lichens present another tasty morsel for the discerning palate. Rocky shore lichens also tend to be flattish chaps that cover the rocks but their domestic set-up is a bit peculiar. Apparently, some time ago, a rebel piece of microscopic algae got pissed off with its algal chums and went off in search of high adventure [last seen catching the number 40 from London, Victoria]. Minutes passed and the algae came upon a non-conformist group of fungi who promptly invited the itinerant in for a heart-to-heart about how boring fungal life can be. Ideas were kicked about (ideas sought guidance from the European Court of Rights) and eventually a union was proposed that would have shocked even the baby-eating bishop of Bath and Wells.

Ever since these two Bohemian groups have been living together in sin, the algal cells inside a nice fungal home, and marriage ceremonies are now available in remote parts of Sweden.

Barnacles.

Barnacles are undoubtedly not the gazelles of the rocky shore. You could scream 'FIRE' 'til your tonsils were tap-dancing all over your forehead but you would not see barnacles sprinting about the place. Last in the Titanic's lifeboats by a mile.

There is a good reason for this. These chaps, when young, float about in the sea just like young limpets do then one day they turn into something resembling a moon-rocket for bacteria. Faced with the option of doing something excitingly extraterrestrial or landing on a rocky shore they choose the latter. Next, they indulge in a curious bit of shuffling about, apparently looking for their mates, and when they find them they move away a bit, as decency dictates, get all cosy and settle down. No doubt all flushed with achievement they then do something rather odd, the young barnacle in question cements its own head to the floor and then sets about constructing a bungalow out of calcium carbonate.

For the rest of their lives, unless aliens invade and turn the rocks into rice pudding or something else unusual happens, they stay glued to the spot no doubt having a massively exciting time. As you may have guessed Thor Heyerdahl did not have barnacle blood running through his well-travelled veins.

It is bad form to poke fun at fellow rocky shore inmates but there are certain features about barnacles that make one roll about. Feeding behaviour is good for a start.

When the tide is out barnacles look for all the world like very small, bored volcanoes. As the water returns word goes around that it is time to do some serious chomping. Erstwhile-bored volcanoes start flexing their plate hinges and suddenly the roofs open up like a battery of missile silos. Feeding appendages are produced [that look like a cross between a clawed hand and a shuttlecock having a nervous breakdown] which wave through the water, catching bits of food as they go. From a distance feeding barnacles look like an assembly of extremely camp male hairdressers, gesticulating wildly after a rousing speech about a revolutionary new hair gel product or something equally important.

After hunger pangs have been attended to our exciting barnacle friends tend to shut up shop and return to bored-volcano mode: that is unless something very nasty happens.

Not all the individuals found on the shore are my pals; one exclusion from the big-buddy club is a fish called the blenny. Calling a blenny a pal would be stretching the definition as much as you would have to stretch a young pea's skin so that it could give planet earth a new green t-shirt.

The blenny has a particularly sour temperament and is about as happy as a Grand National winner that has just been told to re-run the course after all its legs have been amputated. Blennies hang around, spitting on the floor, leering at young girls and playing loud music until barnacle feeding time. When the barnacles have got their bits out the blennies zap up and bite them off. This leaves the poor old barnacle waving a totally useless stump about until the Grim Reaper pops round with a measuring tape.

Rather a sorry state of affairs if you ask me.

Barnacle reproductive antics deserve a mention. Imagine the problem. Your head is cemented to the floor and impenetrable walls surround you, you are madly in love with the barnacle just down the rocks that is in a similar predicament. You have both decided that you wish to make little barnacles as soon as possible and have communicated this to each other using strange and mysterious barnacle channels.

There are (surprisingly) a number of options. One, join the Foreign Legion; two, shove your reproductive materials into the water and hope for the best (the method favoured by yours truly); three, at least one half of the partnership has to be in possession of a bit of a whopper. Big enough to bridge the gap between you and your intended and make the rocky shore move [as in 'Did the rocky shore move for you darling?' to which the reply is 'Absolutely darling.'].

Well barnacles have plonked, if you'll excuse the term, for the third option. Option one was rejected because barnacles are not renowned for their ability to march across miles of desert in a bizarre hat. Option two got the elbow, as it simply wasn't enough fun and that left option three.

The solution to the barnacle dilemma is an impressive one. If barnacles were magnified up to human proportions they would be the proud owners of male reproductive organs the size of Nelson's Column. The down side is they wouldn't be buying trousers off the peg. You might think the presence of such a massive appendage would impart supreme manliness to its owner but in reality barnacles can be chaps and girls at the same time. If you need to refer to this state of affairs in polite company the technical term is 'simultaneous hermaphrodites'. If the company is not so fussy then 'screaming perverts' will probably do just as well.

Incidentally the Nelson's Column statistic is well documented. Years ago a fanatical cell of Luddite terrorists had developed a weapon to magnify Intel computer chips up to the size of dinner tables. Unfortunately, during tests, they accidentally hit a barnacle and the terrorists, who as fate would have it were nuns, all died of shock. The affected barnacle went on to become something of a celebrity [it was invited to join the Big Brother house but wasn't that desperate] though in the end got tired of intrusive pictures in the Tabloids and getting it out for the girls.

Topshells and periwinkles.

If you have ever wandered around on the rocky shore and wondered what the little snail like chaps were, topshells and periwinkles is probably the answer to your question. These are my best pals in the world and the chaps I have most in common with. I'm not being 'ovinist' when I say that what we are dealing with here is the sheep of the inter-tidal zone. Like me these chaps are solid vegetarians to a man and get their sustenance by dragging their tongues over the floor, in short they follow the same diet plan as yours truly.

When we are out of our shells [as in 'wandering about' not as in 'a drug induced stupor'], limpets, topshells and periwinkles are jolly similar. This can cause a certain amount of confusion when it is time to get back into one's shell again.

Some of the molluscan youth have these shell-swapping parties when the really big high and low tides happen in spring and autumn. They get over exited and swap shells in a rebellious frenzy. They then drive the new shell around the shore at high speed, frightening young prawns and confusing the crap out of their parents. It always ends in tears.

Now why on earth would we leave the safety of our shells? I hear you mutter [alternatively you might be reading this as some form of punishment and don't really give a stuff]. Well I'll tell you anyway and if you are reading this under sufferance that's just tough-titties.

Well us adults leave the safety of our shells but once a year. No human has ever seen this happen so don't be surprised if disbelieving experts pooh-pooh the whole thing when you gush excitedly all over them at the next malacalogical society conference. Over the course of a year certain body parts get a bit soiled. Old food and other less socially acceptable items tend to pile up and things get a bit itchy and scratchy. It is therefore necessary, in the interests of hygiene and social continuity, to have a damn good wash to cleanse the bits that don't usually get done.

Needless to say we have to be very careful about when we do this. Sunny days are right out or we would end up looking like a Jelly-Baby that had spent the last four billion years sitting in a deck chair in the Sahara desert. Winter is risky as it can be damned difficult coaxing a, once soft and squidgy, body back into its shell when it has achieved the consistency of a Foxes' Glacier Mint.

Hundreds of naked snails leaping about the shore with something approaching gay abandon encourages motion-envy in sessile species (barnacles are the worst) and also attracts the feathered brigade to come down and have a stuff-a-crop party.

The only option is to pick a warm autumn evening, when there is no moonlight for the gulls to see us by, so this is what we do. Winkles, topshells and limpets as naked as completely naked things having a good old frolic in the surf until the corpus is as clean as Beyonce's floor. Her floor that is, after a visit from the 'Flash' representative to whom she had said, 'Clean my floor thoroughly, big boy, and if it's clean enough you can do anything you like to my naked body as long as it doesn't involve complex algebra.'

CALL THIS A SHELL?

EDIBLE P. W.

Then completely refreshed we climb back into our freshly scrubbed shell (a service performed by the shell-fairies), go home and have a power nap. Even dogwhelks join in with this yearly ritual; everyone is rather nervous about this at first (for reasons that will become apparent later) but they always honour the truce and even a voracious carnivore needs a bath once in a while.

Lumping topshells and periwinkles together, as we have done so far, might give the impression that they are very similar and might as well be called 'topples' or something. Well this is not the case. Even though, like moi, they are guilty as hell of being rocky shore snails there are differences and if you are one of the aforementioned they are important ones. I'm afraid we are back to the delicate subject of sex again.

Oh, goodie.

Topshells are neatly divided up into males and females [putting limpets on rather a black-sheep footing incidentally] and so are the jolly old periwinkles. No massive differences so far but in the event that a winkle fancied playing 'hide the sausage' with a young lady topshell there would be some pretty red faces about after the seduction scene. Winkles copulate but topshells, like limpets, avail themselves of the briny for the gametes coming-out party, in other words they shove everything out into the water and hope for the best. Bodily contact in topshells is about as socially acceptable as turning up to a Buckingham Palace garden party dressed like Osama bin Laden.

Still topshells, even bohemian ones, are very unlikely to be caught *in flagrante delicto* with a winkle as they are rather snooty and think themselves rather superior to the lower winkle orders: all because of a bit of mother-of-pearl.

If you happen to be on a rocky shore and are extremely bored, as you might be during a game of chess with a breezeblock, pick up a topshell and have a look at the bit around the hole where the animal you have just frightened to death has disappeared. It's the bit that topshells are really proud of; all around the shell opening is a rather splendid patch of mother-of-pearl.

Damned pretty.

Trouble is they get all egotistical about it and flaunt their evolutionary good fortune all over young impressionable winkles. The poor old winkles end up feeling desperately inadequate and some of them grow up to be serial killers.

Tubeworms.

I have to mention tubeworms really but there is not a lot to say. If you have ever pottered about on the shore and have been puzzled by the little squiggly white bits on the rocks and some seaweeds then you have seen tubeworms, you have been there and done that.

They live in calcium carbonate houses [don't we all?], but the houses look as if something went horribly wrong at the planning stage: because it did.

Incidentally this calcium carbonate stuff has cropped up a number of times and you might not know what it is. Basically it is an extremely close relative of chalk. So close that if 'chalk' had been found guilty of putting magic mushrooms in the 'soup of the day' in the House of Lords' canteen, then 'calcium carbonate' would be doing ten years in the nearest penitentiary: that close.

Anyway the plans for these houses were sitting on the architect's desk while he had nipped off for a slug (strange expression that) of gin and tonic. While he was away a dwarf from catering college leapt in through the window (this happened all the time apparently) equipped with one of those slightly suspect conical bags that chefs ice cakes with.

The dwarf went artistically berserk all over the plans with white icing (another common but rather odd occurrence), the architect, on his return, was too pissed to notice, submitted the plans and another monstrous carbuncle made it through to the construction stage.

Still the tubeworms seem perfectly happy with the arrangement and there must be a vindictive dwarf (possibly a chef by now) somewhere who is missing out on royalties.

Other fascinating facts about tubeworms? There aren't any. They just sit around in their tubes, smiling in a sickeningly contented way, occasionally erecting something that looks like an umbrella without the canvas bit into the water to catch unwary bits of food.

Well to be honest I have lied to you, there is something else about tubeworms that I have omitted simply because I am too embarrassed to commit it to the printed page. It's one thing to know something sordid is going on but quite another to put it into words. I'm afraid we are back to sex again but this time, oh my tentacles it's rude.

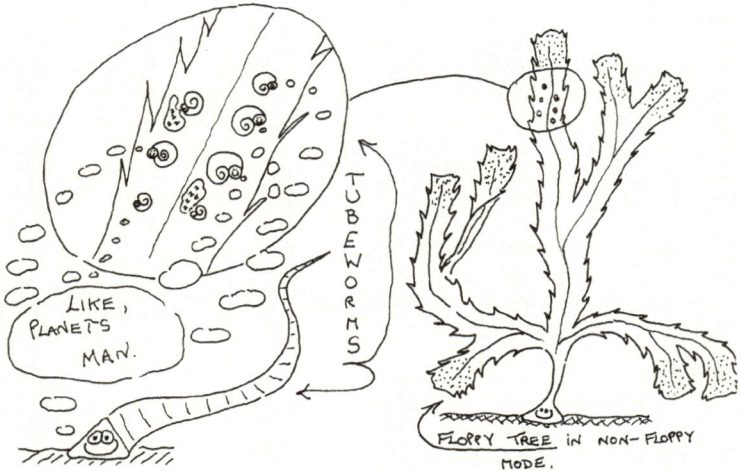

FLOPPY TREE IN NON-FLOPPY MODE.

Tubeworms are somewhat in sympathy, I blush to say, with us limpets as they pop their gametes into the water. These fuse to form little swimming jobs and after a couple of weeks swanking about in Gaia's maternal fluids they do the decent thing and hit the rocky shore.

Some tubeworms also share this rather embarrassing habit of being chaps first and girls second and far be it from me to criticise them for that little evolutionary quirk. What I simply can't cope with is that they are shameless exhibitionists from the word go. As soon as they land on the shore they secrete this liquid which forms a see-through tube, they inhabit this and just sit there with all their bits on display, flaunting their young bodies to all and sundry: it's a disgrace.

They might as well hang a 'Get it here' notice outside and have done with it. As you might have guessed it brings nothing but trouble. Some of them, at the tender age of four months, are ready [gasping probably] to have babies [too much time hanging around in amusement arcades I suspect]. Still it serves them right as many of them die before even making it as far as their second birthday, they'd be far too shagged out to even contemplate the rigours of adolescence.

Sponges, sea mats, hydroids and sea squirts.

It may seem rather rude to lump these assorted jobs under one heading like the '... and everyone else, you know who you are (which is just as well because I'm buggered if I can remember)' category at awards ceremonies.

Inclusion under this heading means you are about as important as anger management classes for lettuces and your name definitely did not spring to mind under the hot studio lights.

Well the reason I have lumped these chaps together is because they are a bit primitive and can't read so as long as nobody tells them they will be none the wiser. If anybody does tell them, incidentally, things will get quite ugly so don't say you haven't been warned. Sorry I must be drinking too much coffee.

It's even a bit difficult to decide whether sponges *et al* are even conscious, like the people who serve you at DIY Centre's. Another problem with these chaps is trying to decide where one individual begins and where the aforesaid individual ends. Striking up animated conversation or attempting deep and meaningful relationships with life forms that don't have discrete boundaries messes with one's inner car park attendant in a big way. Psychotherapy nothing, we are talking complete rebuild here,

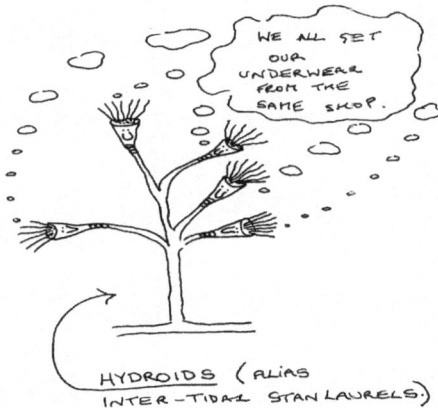

HYDROIDS (ALIAS
INTER-TIDAL STAN LAURELS.)

If you are the proud owner of a spider plant (you need to get a life) but you may know what I mean. There the plant sits for weeks on end doing absolutely nothing, except to look a trifle sad when short of water. One day, when you have just about given up on 'Old Spidey', a little shoot pops out from its mysterious green depths. This projection launches itself boldly out into the world and soon a little green hairstyle appears on the end which turns out to be another spider plant. Or does it?

Is this new and exciting addition to *Le Famille Photosynthetique* another individual or just an offshoot of the old one? Suddenly one is plunged into deep philosophical water without a paddle. The worms are out of the can and somebody forgot the recall signal.

Well it's just like that with sponges and the rest of the gang and that's why I lump them together because they seem quite happy that way.

God that must be one of the longest excuses in history.

Not surprisingly I don't know an awful lot about these guys, they just seem to sit there contemplating Gaia's mystical naval. Life's rich tapestry seems a bit threadbare in the sponge department and I don't think the other compadres are any better off. Sometimes they get a bit animated and thrash about when the tide comes in to collect food, occasionally they go a little wild and release the old reproductive bits and pieces (to ensure there will be offspring to confuse future generations). But as far as an outsider can tell that is essentially IT.

Are they really happy? Is that a smile on their faces or is it just flatulence? Have they achieved the Nirvanic Big One or are they just terribly, terribly tedious?

Sorry I ramble.

Dogwhelks.

Stripping the descriptive problem down to its underpants you could quite truthfully say that dogwhelks are white snails and they are about the same size as a jumper that has spent the last forty years in a tumble dryer (hot cycle) and is now approximately the same size as a thimble. Unfortunately dogwhelks can be just about any colour under the sun and the descriptive problem does not take kindly to being in its smalls in public and starts throwing on layers like a piece of grit in a rabid oyster's shell. Still, you get the general idea.

Describing a dogwhelk as a pal is rather like calling the 'News of the World' a newspaper. It's such an inaccurate description that if a similar mistake had been made with Kevin the Killer Elephant's publicity poster audiences would have been trampled to death while looking for a beetle dressed like Beatrix Potter.

Dogwhelks eat barnacles. They also eat mussels, topshells, winkles and even, God forbid, limpets. It's not so much being eaten that is the problem, when your time is up your time is up, it's the way you get eaten that is so grizzly.
A dogwhelk will creep up on a barnacle (an unnecessary precaution as the barnacle isn't exactly going anywhere) and what happens next is quite impressive if you if you enjoy chainsaw massacres.

The dogwhelk produces its tongue.

Yes I can see you rolling around in terror with eyes bulging at the sockets. Well this tongue has got the edge on most when it comes to getting display space in the chamber of horrors. It is called an 'accessory boring organ' and this has nothing to do with how interesting it is. Basically it bores through the shell of its victim having softened things up a bit with an enzyme or two. The men from Black & Decker have recently been seen taking dogwhelks to expensive seafood restaurants and eavesdroppers have heard the words 'patent' and 'filthy rich' whispered a few times.

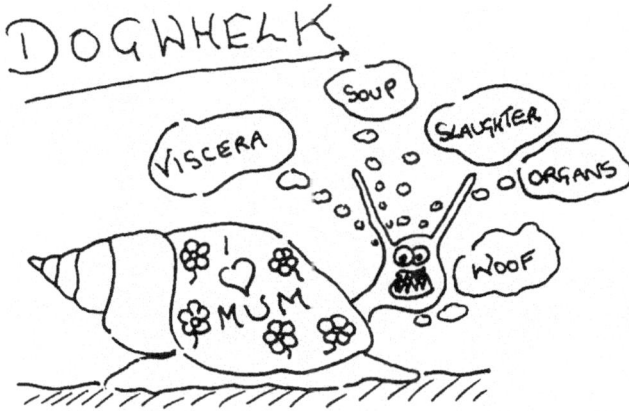

Then things get slightly worse for the poor old barnacle. It is paralysed by a narcotic and is forced to sit there and watch while slowly but surely it is turned into barnacle soup. This double dose of unpleasantness is a bit like being attacked by Martians and, just as you decide to surrender, their mates from Uranus turn up (in a really bad mood as they have just heard about the rude double meaning of their planet's name) and they are in no mood to take hostages.

In short you are buggered.

Buggered in the same way that a beautifully crafted rice paper model of the Hanging Gardens of Babylon would be if placed in the path of a teetotal hippopotamus that had just been force fed twenty pints of Ted Tickle's viscera emulsifying special brew.

After soup-like rendering has occurred the dogwhelk sucks liquid barnacle up and presumably strolls off to look for another victim. It is scant consolation to know that dogwhelks are eaten by crabs and are therefore unlikely to become planetary overlords.

Having dealt with the rather gory process of feeding it is high time to revisit smut city.

Come springtime, when the sap is rising in portions of the molluscan world, these walking [well sliding really] food processors smooth down the shore for what amounts to a massive orgy. Clothes are strewn liberally about the place and a scene that would have shocked Caligula's aunty ensues. Dogwhelks are fairly straightforward sort of chaps in that the chaps are chaps for life and the girls are girls [tabloid press rattle back to the office, tails between legs].

However the male dogwhelk's reproductive apparatus is a subject for sustained merriment [tabloid reporters rattle back again, grinning maniacally]. If you imagine the most amusing place for a sizeable willie to be found you will only be wrong by a whisker, it is located just behind the right hand side of a dogwhelk's head, easily close enough for plenty of ribald jokes and appropriate nicknames roughly approximating to 'Richard Head'.

Anyway the chaps shimmy around the shore, waving their amusing willies about, driving the girls wild and copulation occurs in no uncertain terms.

Post-coital female dogwhelks, instead of retiring quietly to an institute for young mothers, doing a bit of knitting and looking up the words 'post' and 'natal' in a dictionary, do a number of things, which might be considered unusual. First, instead of producing a squealing, pink bundle of joy, they slide off to the nearest crevice and lay a whole load of egg-capsules. Second, the dogwhelk young mothers' association show devotion to duty in a rather impressive fashion. Instead of catching the nearest plane to Barbados for a post-natal soak in the sun, they plunge straight back into the continuing orgiastic fray to try for more babies. This behaviour shows tremendous tenacity and pluck or alternatively, a rather overly healthy appetite for a spot of rumpy-pumpy.

Meanwhile, back at the capsules [now there's a phrase that doesn't get used enough] things are starting to happen. These capsules look a little bit like yellow skittles that have been shrunk for use by the local grasshopper league. Inside these mysterious vessels there are a lot of little eggs that are sulking because they didn't get fertilised, mixed in with these are a few pretty smug, fertilised eggs, which in the fullness of time hatch to allow miniature dogwhelks to escape.

Miniature dogwhelks hold to the same philosophy as the adults and add insult to injury by chomping their way through their infertile siblings. Having ransacked the egg capsule for sustenance they then go off and terrorise young barnacles. Anything that gets in the way is likely to be liquidised before it can say, 'Hey look man, like why can't we all be vegetarian, ok?' and the small carnivorous thugs carry on like this until they become big carnivorous thugs.

It's a great comfort to know that dogwhelks are so rabid in their carnivory that they resort to cannibalism at the drop of a hat, unfortunately not enough hats are dropped on the shore to make this a reassuring insurance policy.

Anemones.

Being a shelled chap myself it is not surprising that most of my chums are in the same chalky boat. However there are a few pals loitering about the shore who are rather deficient in the outer garment department, sadly lacking in the calcium carbonate body armour stakes, in fact they are as naked as streakers at a streakers' convention going for the 'Streaker of the year' award. Anemones fall into this category right up to their metaphorical eyeballs.

There are many different kinds of anemone but there is one type that is particularly common on the shore; ladies and gentlemen I refer to none other than the beadlet anemone [insert small drum roll here if desired].

You may have spotted these little guys if you have strolled about on rocky shores. If you have strolled about on rocky shores incidentally you sound a little too cool for your own good. I suspect you were only pretending to be cool when in fact you were scared nipple-less about falling to a messy death and committing social suicide at the same time. Anyway you may have seen something on the rocks that looks like someone has discarded an American hard gum, in the early stages of its demise. Blackcurrant flavour I think. Well these are beadlet anemones.

I suppose another way to describe the beadlet buddy is to say it's like the dome of St. Paul's Cathedral converted to blackcurrant jelly and miniaturised for use as a suppository for a chimpanzee, that sort of thing. I hope that has helped.

Now you might be concerned that Larry has gone a bit senile here, too much aluminium in the cooking pots, woof woof, wheep wheeeeeeep. Anemones have tentacles sticking out of their topknots, St. Paul's cathedral, even after blackcurrant jelly conversion, does not. You may be wondering why you are reading this garbage especially now the situation has deteriorated because the author has gone bananas.

Well I shall explain.

My pal the beadlet has a cunning trick up its many sleeves. One of the problems with not owning a shell is that when the tide goes out, and rocky shore denizens start holding on to water like it was a chastity belt and the Vikings are on the way, it's difficult not to dry out and end up looking like a baby that has just spent the last epoch or two in a salty Jacuzzi.

If you have got lots of tentacles and you wave them about in the sunlight, as you might do in panic because your Caribbean cruise liner has hit a rock and is sinking fast, odds on you'd be as dry as an alcoholic's drinks cabinet before the lifeboats arrived. But if you tuck all your tentacles into the middle of your body and wait until the tide comes in again you will be laughing all the way to the Desert Rats' reunion dinner.

Feeding time for the beadlet is an interesting affair.

Consider a shrimp, having a frightfully ripping afternoon pottering about in a rockpool, wondering if John and Yoko would have recognised each other with their clothes on. Suddenly it spies something looking like a tree that has been attacked by killer tomatoes and jets over to investigate.

Curiosity being what it is [a rather strange, furry animal with unblinking eyes and nostrils the size of the channel tunnel] the shrimp gently nudges one of the trees 'branches', promptly gets an Exocet missile in the groin and dies before it can utter "Sod it, I thought that only applied to cats". Basically this is how an anemone gets its man. As soon as some unsuspecting passer-by touches one of the tentacles they get stung and paralysed. From then on the anemone casually pulls bits off the obliging stiff, passes them to its mouth [actually a multi-purpose orifice it uses to pooh with as well - thank God for evolution] and assimilates as appropriate. I suppose "Thank God for evolution" opens up a bit of a can of worms philosophically speaking, rumours will spread that limpets subscribe to the idea of 'intelligent design', well you never could keep rumours under control.

Beadlets have babies in a slightly different fashion to most anemones.

Many of the tentacled multitude reproduce by splitting in two. One minute there is Arnold the Anemone telling the joke about the vicar and the waste disposal unit, next minute Arny seems to have forgotten the punch line and now [after a titanic struggle inside his dinner jacket which eventually explodes, throwing bits of satin lining over a wide area] wishes to be known as Freddie and Frederick, the Fission Twins.

Difficult sort of behaviour to cope with in the best of circumstances but a nightmare if you are hosting a dinner party and it happens to one of your guests. Dreams of the social event of the year turn to ashes as you are a lemon sorbet short and there aren't enough coffee cups to go round.

Fortunately beadlets make safer dinner guests than most anemones, as they don't go in for this sort of behaviour. The female sits there coyly in an 'I'm waiting to be fertilised' sort of way. The male, driven wild by this display of coyness, hurls lumberjack type particles into the water with instructions to go to the female, go directly to the female, do not pass go and do not collect two hundred pounds. The female does the decent thing and lets the small reproductive chaps in, allows them to ravish her eggs and after a bit of a pregnant pause gives birth to perfectly formed baby beadlets. These baby beadlets are so tiny that you could fit fifteen billion of them on a pinhead and still not have room for an aircraft carrier. They are so sweet and cuddly that if you made an aerosol from "baby beadlet" sweetness and sprayed it all over the world there would be no more wars and even terrorists might stop blowing innocent people up for having different opinions about stuff.

Well at least that is how it goes in the storybooks. To be honest, the way that beadlets produce babies is still a bit of a mystery. It appears that the girls and the chaps may brood babies inside them, how the babies get inside the chaps is anybodies guess. Mysterious processes like 'internal budding' and 'parthenogenesis' may be involved but being a simple limpet I haven't a bloody clue what this means.

It is also possible that anemones are squidgy gateways to other universes and their babies are cunningly disguised alien killing machines just waiting until Superman is on holiday before taking over the planet.

Shore crabs.

Although this little number is called 'Larry and his Pals' I ought to say that this title is not one hundred percent accurate. I have already hinted that dogwhelks are not exactly popping round for bedtime Cocoa and a cosy chat; difficult to share confidences with something that might turn you into limpet soup if there's a lull in the conversation. Luckily dogwhelks are stupid, probably as a result of the positioning of their willie, and if you disguise yourself with a bit of seaweed on the roof of the house they usually slide straight past having mistaken you for a bit of the rocky shore.

Crabs are much worse.

Their lust for violence is only matched by that of the little known son of Genghis Khan, who was put to death at the age of three, by his own father, for being too nasty. I only give an account of these vile additions to the animal kingdom so that the reader can look away disdainfully if she or he is ever introduced.

Like a lot of my real pals crabs start life in the plankton but they start as little larval delinquents. By the time they have floated around for a short time they have usually been thrown out of nightclubs for molesting young prawns and beating juvenile barnacles over the head with beer bottles.

Then they change into another larval stage. This is distinguishable from the previous stage by being even nastier and more thug-like. By the time they have changed into young crabs things have really deteriorated. Most of them have criminal records as long as Elastoman's legs after he tried hanging from the guttering of the Empire State Building with his new lead boots on.

It's not even as if they grow out of it. On the rocky shore, having caused havoc in the plankton, adolescent male (is their a worse developmental stage anywhere in the animal kingdom?) crabs loiter around in gangs under boulders and seaweed threatening young topshells and winkles with sawn off razorshell fragments. They are habitually high on squid ink derivatives, don't shave for days on end and never wash under their ten armpits.

The girls are no better. Mincing about seductively in vinyl miniskirts and black fishnet stockings (the latter they manufacture themselves by flattening young sand eels with rocks). They deliberately stick their stiletto heels through the sides of poor anemones, making them leak.

I blame the parents. They simply don't care what the young crabs get up to, if anything they encourage them. Many years ago, when I was moving home for the first time, I met an unusual young shore crab that wished to become a Buddhist monk. The poor chap was dressed up in rotting seaweed and hanging from a bit of driftwood at the time, a clear sign of his so-called 'mates' disapproval.

Eventually a seagull came and ate him.

Hopefully his 'mates' will reincarnate as extremely pathetic winkles in the next life and suffer a hideous fate.

Before long the inevitable happens (as it would of course). Male and female crabs go off for some mischief behind the boulders, then it's all tears when the female discovers she can't get into her mini-skirt any more because her brood pouch is too big. Eventually the eggs hatch to produce another generation of planktonic reprobates.

Oh God.

Crab's eating habits are a disgrace. They'll eat anything that moves and if it doesn't move they have probably eaten it already. They rip food apart with a set of pincers that would not look out of place in the 'Big Stuff' section of a Screwfix catalogue. In the four and a half billion years that God has been trying to decide whether planet earth was a mistake a crab has never used a napkin or said thank you; the excuse that they did not evolve until millions of years later is simply not good enough.

There is nothing like a good rant is there?

I don't wish to give the impression that all crabs are like this. There are some extremely well mannered porcelain crabs and hermit crabs so to redress the balance slightly I'll tell you about them.

Porcelain crabs are small, home-loving vegetarians that hide shyly under stones spending their days crocheting and reciting poetry. The only slightly strange facet about porcelain crabs is that they look as if the parts department supplied them with the wrong pincers. A similar effect would be achieved by sticking Arnold Schwarzenegger's arms on a small child.

Hermit crabs seem to spend their days hunting for bizarre objects to hide inside and call home. As they get bigger they have to find progressively larger containers to accommodate them, the oldest hermit crab alive, old 'Henry Mc. Huge' up in Sullom Voe, in the Shetland Isles, now uses a discarded super tanker as a weekend cottage.

Starfish.

In the line of duty I feel obliged to mention starfish but it gives me no pleasure. You may remember the potential embarrassment involved in having anemones to dinner, a guest undergoing binary fission halfway through the first course does tend to put guests off their pudding a tadge. At least you might have invited them in the first place.

Nobody in their right minds would invite a starfish to a dinner party.

Their favourite food is mussels and I suppose you can't really condemn a man to solitary confinement for that, heaven for me is a succulent patch of green seaweed but that's beside the point. I think the problem arises in the etiquette department.

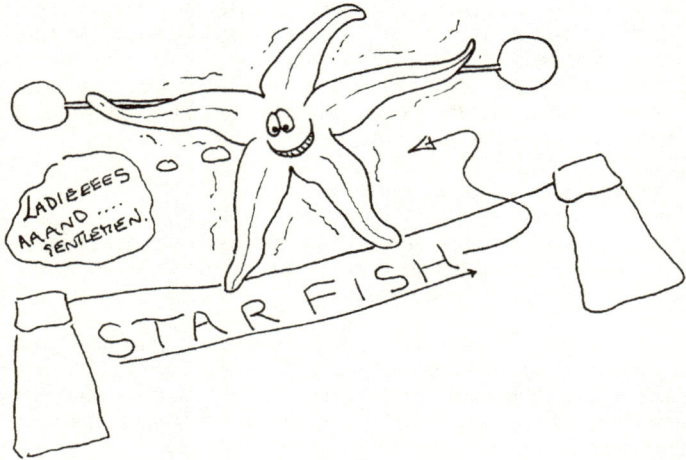

They sidle up to their prospective meal and using a couple of arms, of which they have an embarrassing richness, they pull the two shells of the unfortunate victim apart. No real social blunders yet I'll grant you, there's nothing desperately wrong with a chap pulling mussels apart in the corner, it's almost reminiscent of a nice evening in with the Simpson's.

But the next stage of the starfish banquet is the equivalent of Marge Simpson pulling out a chainsaw and hacking her way gleefully through the other family members.

The starfish ejects its own stomach into the gap it has created chez mussel and proceeds to digest our bivalvian chums' organs externally. Eventually the whole shooting match is sucked back in while helpless onlookers vomit noisily into the buckets provided.

It's difficult to cope with the idea of a dinner party where after the pre-prandial sherry and gentle banter about whether Michael Jackson has got any of his original body parts left at all, everyone settles down to the soup course and at the appropriate moment a bevy of stomachs shoot out and land in the bowls, pulsating gently.

God the laundry bills.

Mussels.

I'd be the first to admit that my accounts of dogwhelks, crabs and starfish were ever so slightly negative so I thought I would finish off with one of my best pals of all, the mussel.

Mussels are wonderful; they don't have any nasty idiosyncratic glitches at all. Like their mates (barnacles) they sit there happily day after day filtering little bits from the water, I've never seen a mussel that wasn't smiling. Unfortunately this could mean that they are somewhat devoid of grey matter (as in thick). I mean who smiles when they are being eaten by a dogwhelk?

God, they might be perverts.

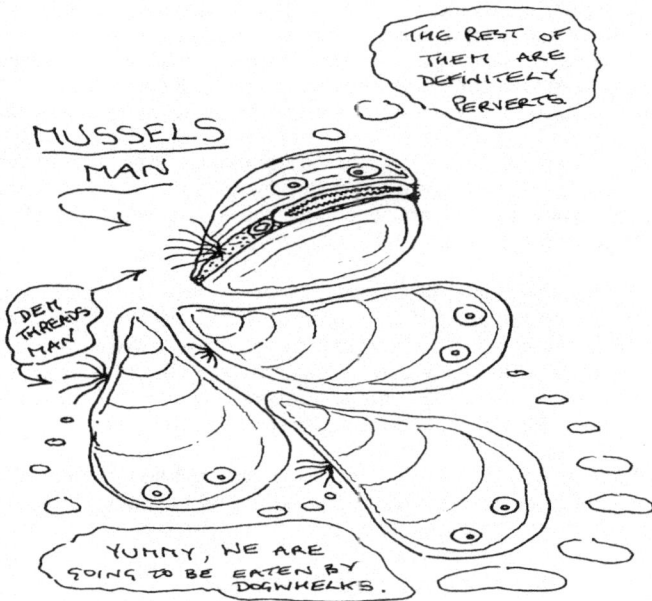

Anyway, that on one side, mussels are spiffing chaps.

A big disadvantage if you are a mussel is that you are big and irresistibly tasty to just about every rocky shore predator that has ever existed. As a direct consequence poor old mussels get hammered by the skunks mentioned above.

But there is always the mussel's revenge.

This terrible revenge only really applies to dogwhelks but perhaps that makes it all the sweeter. Mussels are attached to the rocks by things called byssus threads, these hold the mussel in place in much the same way that a tent is anchored by its ropes and pegs. Instead of having little pegs at the bottom though byssus threads have suckers. Now the cunning part is that when old 'Richard Head' comes-a-hunting apparently helpless mussels they latch on to him (or her) with their threads and cling on for dear life. 'Tricky Dicky' (a now rather useless, supine food processor) now has the thrilling opportunity to contemplate the cosmic order of things until he (or she) joins the carnivorous choir celestial, pushes up the seaweeds, gets to meet his (or her) maker etc.

Mussels have a pretty static time as adults but they certainly make up for it by having a fairly racy youth in which they spend a lot of their time mimicking their favourite super-hero, Spiderman.

After zapping around in the plankton for a few weeks they settle on young, innocent bits of seaweed where they flirt with the idea of attachment, slinging the odd byssus or two out in a teasing fashion. Just as the seaweed has become resigned to accommodating a hitchhiker for the foreseeable future the young mussel zaps off into the deep and blue to do its Spiderman impression.

These little chaps produce a long thread from which they hang in the water. Molluscan poets, of which there are a surprising number, have described this bit of dare-devilry as the equivalent of 'the gossamer flight of spiders'. Molluscan poets are obviously complete cretins.

These little hanging Spidermen are not called mussels at this point, they are referred to as 'plantigrades', this is a bit of a mystery to me as I thought a plantigrade was something you sorted potatoes out with (especially if they had been naughty and needed a good tweaking). Still after a taste of the open road, a different city every night, the shell eventually gets to them and, just like us limpets, they settle down to domestic bliss on the rocky shore.

Well that has introduced you to most of my pals and some of the other, less desirable, elements that we have to live with. Now I suppose I had better tell you why I'm writing this in the first place.

3. Why Larry might be wasting his time.

It is unusual for a limpet to write his memoirs but I felt compelled to as I think I might be dying.

My pals are also looking a little pasty and I just wanted to make sure there is an accurate record of what life used to be like on the rocky shore. Nobody may care but they can't scoff at a chap for trying.

It was funny at first. The male dogwhelks, who nobody really liked anyway, gathered for their spring orgy, looking disgustingly fit and healthy as usual but when the ladies turned up lustful grins faded and a general muttering ensued, there was even an attempt at a wailing and gnashing of non-existent teeth.

The ladies appeared to have grown what can only be described as a willie.

We all rolled about of course as the dogwhelks dispersed having given the old reproductive bash a bit of a miss. Some of the elders of the dogwhelk community were carted off to the nearest defibrillators, just in case, and were overheard muttering that it wasn't a good sign when girls grew willies. Difficult to disagree with that really. Female dogwhelks with reproductive extras just isn't on.

Rumour had it that a chemical in the water caused the females' embarrassment but you never can tell.

Another strange phenomenon was the increase in the number of bits in the water. The filter feeders went bonkers of course; increased smugness amongst the tubeworm fraternity was noted and even sponges showed brief flashes of animation. Some of the seaweeds complained about lack of light but they always whinged anyway and were studiously ignored. Dark mutterings about the "bloody vegetation complaining again" were overheard but soon hushed up for fear of a good threshing when the next tide came in.

The bits kept on appearing though and some over enthusiastic tube worms outgrew their tubes, which led to embarrassment and some indecent exposure charges.

We were used to looking on the sea as a friend, it always replenished food supplies, provided a nice drink and for us limpets was the vital fluid allowing baby limpets to be produced.

The sea could do no wrong.

Occasionally bits of plastic would drift in, it was quite good fun reading the writing on the side to see where it originated but sometimes the birds would choke on it or get it tangled round their legs, afterwards their legs would go a funny colour and fall off. Sometimes birds would get tied to the ground and starve to death.

Then things got really worrying.

One day the sea came in and brought a thin film of shiny stuff on its surface. When it washed past us it burnt so we clamped down tight until it went away again: nothing too bad really. Some older, slower limpets didn't clamp down in time and dropped off the rocks, that was quite sad and worrying, nobody seemed to know what was going wrong.

Then yesterday, as the sea advanced it brought in so much of the burning stuff with it that it coated everything. Even when the sea went out our homes were still black. Lots of my pals died and birds were crashing about nearby complaining that their stomachs were burning and they didn't seem to be able to float any more. It was all rather frightening.

Well I was getting a bit knackered from holding on so tight. The next high tide brought even more of the burning stuff with it so I thought I'd better write this stuff down and stick this rather long message in a bottle.

Maybe someone will find it and send some help.

Probably as you read this though Larry and his pals may well be dead.

THE END OF PART, THE FIRST.

Volume two: Larry goes on holiday by mistake.

1. Larry departs.

Hello there.

I didn't die after all. (Gasps of relief from the faithful few who ploughed their way through the first volume of my memoirs). Mind you it was a phenomenally close shave. A novelty balloon drifting off course and nearly landing in the middle of a porcupine's annual picnic might know a thing or two about how close.

If you did miss the excitement of the first volume, a recap might be useful.

Larry, as in moi, gave a riveting, blow-by-blow account of his life to date and a no holds barred account of limpetdom, including all the smut. Larry, still as in moi, then proceeded to rattle on about his chums on the rocky shore and some of the less desirable members of the shore community were given as brief an airing as possible, for completeness that is.

By all accounts it was a roller coaster (or do I mean beer-mat?) of a novel; a tour de force that set the author firmly on the throne next to, the now extremely decomposed, Tolkein and kept him there. Grannies were known to have turned a thousand-wash underwear-grey at some of the lurid disclosures and small children were locked in their rooms, blindfolded, while adults checked the suitability of the material. Potatoes, courgettes and sensitive types of fruit decomposed rapidly when certain passages were read out loud and a number of household pets became incontinent when exposed to some of the ruder passages.

Even so the book became something of a cult classic. Some of the more culturally impoverished countries in Eastern Europe flirted with the idea of adopting limpets as their national emblems. Special hats were designed and large grants became available for new buildings with dome shaped roofs.

BUT all in all, people were worried.

At the end of the account, (when, usually, the bad eggs have been ritually disembowelled with a crochet needle and the hero has smoothed off into the sunset with some rampant tot), all was not well with our hero. I was suffering from a fairly severe bout of oil pollution and was about as vital and full of beans as Superman after colonic irrigation with finest quality Kryptonite.

In the days that followed I discovered that an oil tanker called the SEA EMPRESS had attempted to surgically implant itself into some cliffs near my home. Quite why it should do this is a bit of a mystery but the words "incompetence" and "low-tide" spring to mind. The net result was that while various parties made the proverbial piss-up in a beer-making establishment look unarrangable, something like 72,000 tonnes of oil were dumped on the rocky shores, offshore islands and sea beds near to where I lived.

Lots of my chums succumbed and mortal coils were shrugged off like rockets at a firework party. I managed to hold out hoping that the cavalry would arrive. Instead of the boys in blue with their mops and fairy liquid however, fate decided to send a seagull. I am not a bitter individual but when it is my turn I am going to send fate to a supermarket on a desert Island, where they only sell Spam and the tinned music is from the special box set of Eurovision Song Contest entries.

Anyway this feathery thug, seeing that I was less oiled than most things on the rocky shore, started tapping on my shell. I was feeling extremely weak at this point, I would have lost an arm wrestling contest with a diseased harvestman spider, and obligingly dropped off the rock. I was expecting a therapeutic wash and brush up from the boys in blue, (I've always thought that sounded hideously painful but I suppose it's OK if it's done by an expert), but to my surprise the next moment I was airborne. I was heading back to this feathery git's nest to provide amusement and sustenance for young thuglets of the herring gull variety.

I suppose I was fortunate that the herring gull did not want to risk internal injuries by swallowing and regurgitating my shell so it opted for the alfresco option for the chick's meal. (I used to think that alfresco meant that you had to eat it naked until somebody kindly explained that you only have to be naked if you are Italian.)

The nest was a good eight miles away from my home, by feathery courier, as this particular seagull lived on an Island called Skomer. The flight from where I lived to where I was probably going to be converted into young seagull was actually rather beautiful but you'll understand that I wasn't in the mood to appreciate a good view. Immanent doom tends to take the edge off one's aesthetic sense.

BUT as the avian swine-beak approached the Island something rather peculiar happened.

There was a loud cracking sound.

To my surprise, one might go as far as to say delight, old feathery guts dropped me. As I fell towards the sparkling blue briny thing below I glanced back and realised what must have happened. The seagull had been picked out for the broken neck of the day award by a peregrine falcon.

I've always admired peregrines. Admittedly you don't get to see flocks of them on the rocky shore but they do have rather a good reputation amongst us inter-tidal denizens. I've muttered before about the problems of being molested by dogwhelks and crabs but I don't think I had a good rant about seagulls. If skuas are the football hooligans of the bird world then herring gulls, lesser black-backed and great black-backed gulls are their very best, slightly less intelligent, friends.

Herring gulls are rather common, as in vulgar, birds. They spend large amounts of their time hurling abuse at each other whilst mincing about on mainland rubbish tips. In between bouts of abuse they rip open black plastic rubbish sacks and eat the contents. When gulls get bored with eating refuse they sometimes loiter about on the shore. If a limpet is feeling off colour and not holding on properly it will find itself getting the full guided tour of an avian digestive system before the napkins are out of the starting blocks.

I'm delighted to report that dining out on discarded morsels from refuse sacks is not without it's pitfalls. The plastic bags that contain the rubbish get rather warm in the sunlight and act as incubators for bacteria and their families. When these feathery retards rip the bags open and gorge away they get a nice dose of food poisoning and die.

Pause for malicious hysterics and to check that the tear ducts are as dry as a hydrophobic sponge's bedroom.

Lesser black-backed gulls (LBB's) are pretty vile beings too. In the character pop charts they would probably occupy the slot below Margaret Thatcher's wig control specialist. Possibly their most undesirable quirk is that they eat each other's children. For the rest of the universe this is actually rather good news as it means LBB's are not going to take over if they are too busy eating each other's offspring, however, this behaviour does not exactly endear this species to the world at large.

LBB's start life as an egg. No shocks there, most birds when backed into a corner would have to admit to belonging to the same calcium carbonate coated club. Eggs are pretty inoffensive coves. No eggs have been convicted of murder. Eggs do not generally wield chain saws in the direction of the nearest bit of irreplaceable tropical rain forest nor do they beat each other up for having the audacity to support a different football team. Some other species would find themselves pink cheeked when submitted to similar questioning.

Baby LBB's are not too bad. Amusingly enough young birds are called chicks. To say chicks convincingly you need to wear an Afro style wig (if your hair isn't already the right consistency); shades (sunglasses, preferably mirrored) and immensely wide flares. The lapels on your chosen jacket should be large enough to walk a small dog around and an echo sounder is useful to locate the bottom of your shirt collar. Roger Moore wore similar outfits, as did some of the baddies in "Live and let die", the film with the most amusing sheriff in the world in it. Oxfam might still be able to supply the right sort of gear if you go to one of the smaller Welsh branches.

Anyway back to the chicks, (honey-child). They tend to do what most chicks do, strut around in a bad tempered fashion demanding more food, sporting hairstyles that even the sex pistols would have found ridiculous. BUT the chicks have a serious flaw; if they don't get eaten they will grow up to become total bastards. You don't realise what these innocent looking eggs or fluffy chicks will turn into until it's too late. It's a bit like buying an adorable mongrel puppy from a car boot sale and when it grows up you find it's actually a yak, or similar. Not that there is anything wrong with yaks in the right place of course but a basement flat in Clapham is not exactly the best habitat for a high altitude herbivore.

Another rather off-putting fact of LBB adult life is that they are far too lazy to get their own food, they prefer to steal it from puffins instead. LBBs dive-bomb the little chaps when they are returning to the burrow with a beak full of the readies. The nearest human equivalent is mugging granny on her way home from Tesco's because you can't be bothered to travel the extra fifty metres to the store yourself. I think that is correct isn't it? There is now a Tesco's, or equivalent, fifty metres away from every house in Britain. That's why people always use cars to get to them. Sorry if that's bollocks but I'm only an archaeogastropod and we don't know about these things.

Unfortunately, on the gull front there is worse to come. The great black-backed gull. In the same character pop charts this vile addition to the feathery multitude would need a ladder and a large telescope to see Margaret Thatcher's wig control specialist. This gull is bigger and nastier than the other two and has party tricks to match.

Party trick number one. Find a puffin and swallow it whole.

Party trick number two. Find a young rabbit and treat it to the same fate as the puffin.

Party trick number three. Find an adult rabbit, realise that party trick number two is not physically possible without incurring severe structural damage, treat it to a free aerial view of Skomer Island and then drop it. Watch as rabbit entropy increases dramatically as it hits the ground and then enjoy leisurely luncheon of dismembered bunny.

Now in case you were wondering why limpets love peregrines so much it is because one of the biggest (and nastiest) things a peregrine has ever killed is a great black-backed gull. I for one have rarely been more delighted by any piece of ornithological trivia than that and consequently raised my non-existent hat to peregrines in general on my way down to the sea.

Next moment there was a bit of a plop as I hit the water.

I would like to have said something dramatic like "a resounding splash" as I hit the water but limpets being what they are, rather small kneecap shaped objects, means that a bit of a plop is all that one can muster up when plunging into the briny at something approaching terminal velocity.

Hitting the water was uncomfortable. If you have water skied, lost your balance and sat down rather heavily while travelling forward at considerable speed, you will know what it feels like to have involuntary salt-water colonic irrigation. That coupled with dodging the Grim Reapers blade by the thickness of a stick insects thermal underwear, cou d be said to have taken the edge off an otherwise perfectly pleasant day.

It's funny what comes to mind when death can be seen laying the table for a cosy dinner for two. I was fully expecting the heavenly throng to start giving it some stick to some suitably ethereal tune. I waited for light to appear at the end of the long dark tunnel. I even steeled myself for the inevitable life review, hoping desperately that they would forget about the incident with the chicken, two small batteries and a feather duster.

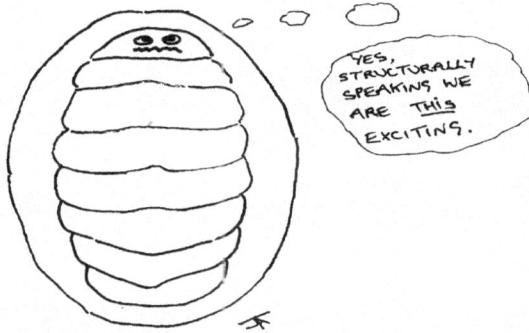

YES, STRUCTURALLY SPEAKING WE ARE THIS EXCITING.

SLIGHTLY MIFFED CHITON ON BEING LEFT OUT OF YOU KNOW WHAT.

Well none of these things occurred. Instead I got a loud and unequivocal "CHITONS."

To which I replied "Oh bugger."

I mean how could I possibly have forgotten Chitons? It's like Laurel going on a world cruise and having arrived safely at Wangdi Phodrang bus station suddenly remembering that he had not seen Hardy since Victoria.

Ridiculous.

Bugger again.

Let me explain. As you are undoubtedly aware by now I am the author of a rather droll little number called "Larry and his pals." This was, and indeed is, a story about Larry (me) and not too unexpectedly, his (my) pals. Bosom buddies like topshells and winkles were included, as the formbooks would have predicted. Even starfish, at decidedly longer odds, got a mention. But chitons were left out.

Does Christopher Robin leave out Winnie the Pooh? Does Wallace go to the moon without Gromit? Does Batman zap off to do bizarre Chiropteran things without Robin?

Does Larry leave Chitons out of his memoirs? Bugger, bugger, bugger.

Yes he bloody well does because he has a punctured watering can for a brain.

Putting chitons in the second volume of my memoirs, which I shall do of course, is the equivalent of trying to saddle up the Derby winner when it has just come out of a tin of dog food. It's just a tadge late.

The dictionary has the cheek to write chitons off as "any small primitive mollusc of the genus Chiton and related genera, having an elongated body covered with eight overlapping shell plates: class Polyplacophora."

Rather confusingly the dictionary also has the cheek to write chitons off as "a loose woollen tunic worn knee length by men and full length by women."

This is not very helpful.

Chitons are a sort of snail, like moi, which looks like a woodlouse that has had all of it's legs removed and has spent the last few years of it's life under ferocious gravitational forces with a rucksack full of stones on it's back. In other words it's vertically challenged, as in rather flat.

Chitons are not primitive at all. They are actually Bodhisattvas that have chosen to shun enlightenment for a while and reincarnate as lowly dorsoventrally flattened molluscs to help us one footed beings reach the nirvanic big one a little sooner. Damn decent of them too.

Also like moi they are vegetarians but they don't tend to go for the same food. As you will remember most seaweeds are soft succulent chaps indulging in frenzied photosynthetic activity until some herbivore bites their bits off. Some members of the algal clan have devised rather a cunning way to cool the average herbivore's digestive ardour. They have packed their little cells with calcium carbonate, the same stuff most of my chums make their shells from, and this makes them about as soft and succulent as the recently discovered last packed lunch of Ramses the third.

Seaweeds of this kind are referred to as "encrusting species" but this may have been distorted, in a Chinese whisper like fashion, from the original version which was "tastes disgusting like faeces". Needless to say most of us plant eating chaps wouldn't touch these encrusting species with a barnacles willy.

The old Bodhisattva chiton brigade wades into this stuff like it was caviar at a Kremlin reunion. They love it. Or do they? Maybe it's an essential part of their spiritual development.

Another riveting piece of information about chitons is that their eight plates articulate. Thankfully this does not mean that they can talk. The sort of conversation one might get out of a chiton's plates would have to be mind bogglingly tedious, chances are they would all speak at once anyway. The articulation business means that (and I quote) they can rear up when disturbed. Well call the media, this is serious news.

I would have thought that when a chiton is disturbed its best strategy would be to lie flat and cling on like merry buggery to the rock surface. The thing that is most likely to disturb a chiton is a crab. Quite how rearing up, when you are close to 20mm long and the thing that has just disturbed you is about ten times the size, will do anything except induce mild hysterics escapes me. Perhaps the chiton strategy is based on the advanced notion that the best way to deal with a voracious predator is to give it a good laugh. Personally I think they overestimate the sophistication of the average crabs sense of humour. A large, obviously very angry, gorilla rearing up would be a fairly effective deterrent, even an extremely p ssed off robin rearing up would be more terrifying.

No, sorry, "chitons rearing up" does not make a lot of sense. Perhaps it just helps them cling to slightly uneven rock surfaces, I must remember to ask them when I get home.

Unfortunately I was distracted from my chitonous musings by a thudlet. I had fallen through something approaching fifteen metres of water when I hit the sandy bottom. The soft sediment cushioned my fall and instantly explained the absence of tunnels of light, life reviews etc., and was rather a relief, albeit in a gritty round the soft underparts sort of way. Still one doesn't like to complain. I'll swap a slight ingress of grit into soft and rather mysterious nether regions for instant death any day. I'll even be prepared to grin maniacally about it in gratitude on national television if called upon to do so. Yes indeed. Hallelujah.

The "thudlet" that may have left you a little perplexed when mentioned above is the best description that I could come up with for the noise I made as I hit the sand. Thud would have overstated the case in the same way that splash would have at the water's surface.

As the sand settled I discovered that I had landed the right way up, (perhaps Sod's Law doesn't operate under water) rear a small rock which was covered with hydroids and bryozoans. If you remember these little colonial chaps got a brief mention in volume one.

Rather disconcertingly Messr's H and B appeared to be chanting and genuflecting like rabid waiters. It took me a long time to get them to stop grovelling and shut up. It took even longer to convince them that just because I had dropped out of the heavens it did not necessarily follow that I was a deity come to lead small colonial animals to their rightful place as rulers of the planet. Admittedly the present planetary overlords seem to be buggering things up a bit but who is to say that hydroids and bryozoans would do any better? Actually it would be rather difficult to imagine them doing any worse.

Having shuffled deification and all it's responsibilities to one side conversation started to flow a bit. Like cold honey. Eventually I found out two interesting bits of information.

1.   I had plopped into the Skomer Marine Nature Reserve, where animals and plants are supposed to be protected and live happily ever after, like pink fluffy bunnies in beautifully clean sea water, and

2.   Most of 1. is total bollocks.

In other words all was not well with the denizens of the deep in this supposed marine haven.

Having had rather a close encounter with the down side of *Homo sapiens'* stewardship of the marine environment myself I decided to speak with someone in authority.

"Take me to your leader" I said as confidently as it's possible to say it with sandy soft parts and post seagull attack syndrome.

"We can't stupid," they said as one. "We are attached to the rocks for the better performance of our duties and anyway we are an autonomous collective. Go to see the Lobster Liberation Front, they'll tell you some stuff that is so horrifying it will deform your tentacles."

Luckily us rocky shore denizens are well versed in the Monty Python archives so I knew perfectly well what an autonomous collective was. All I needed was some instructions as to how the hell one gets to talk to the Lobster Liberation Front, henceforth to be known as the LLF. (Or we shall all get rather fed up with that particular collection of words, won't we?)

Directions obtained I tootled off on the next leg of my journey (maybe foot would have been a better word) with a helpful following current. It has to be said that I was as excited as a small furry animal, at its birthday party, that had accidentally been plugged into the mains.

Obviously you don't get direct instructions to the front door of an underwater terrorist organisation's hideaway; you get the first contact. Mine was a sea fan called Albert who lived a short distance away from the colonial chaps.

Sea fans look a bit like a two dimensional tree, all the branches are in one plane, but they are in fact animals. Lots of animals. As I got closer to Albert I discovered that he was another colonial chap made up of thousands of anemone like bodies.

My original plan, now in tatters, was to sneak up to old Albert in a conspiratorial fashion and quietly enquire about the next step on my journey. I was now at rather a loss as to which "Albert" to ask and since "he" was about 30cm across and as many centimetres high and the current was still running (like the nose of an anteater with hay fever) this might have involved shouting.

Hardly an auspicious start to my career as a secret agent. James Bond could hardly have started more shakily if he had burst into a Women's Institute meeting, with a large megaphone and an inflatable pig on his head, shouting "Hi girls, has anybody seen Felix?" and then Felix rather sheepishly appeared from behind the piano in a nice Marks and Spencer twin set, only to be gunned down by the vicar's wife who was in fact a SPECTRE agent, named Wolfgang, in heavy disguise.

Not a great start but help was at hand. I sidled up to the nearest Albert unit and enquired whom I might need to speak to. To my relief I discovered that all the little Alberts were connected telepathically that in effect made them into a big Albert I didn't have to shout at.

I introduced myself and briefly summarised why a limpet was mincing around in the Skomer MNR. Albert introduced him/themselves and told me a bit about being a sea fan.

This involved quite a bit of stuff about internal skeletons and a mysterious substance called gorgonin. Confusion reigned for a short time because I could have sworn Albert had said something about Gordon's Gin and I had thanked him very much and said that I was rather a fan of Tequila. Albert then got rather confused as to why I was suddenly talking **about** fans when I was already talking **to** one and basically it all started to go horribly wrong.

Eventually this conversational mess was sorted out and I found out that gorgonin was something that all the little Alberts had inside them enabling them to imitate a tree without falling to bits.

Rather depressingly I also found out that Albert did not have the slightest idea where the LLF were hanging out but he did know somebody that did. Instructions were issued and I was informed that my next contact would be a Ross coral. To my surprise and horror the instructions were delivered loudly, by all the little Alberts in close harmony, to the tune of "How do you solve a problem like Maria?" from the Sound of Music.

The effect of this on the local marine fauna and flora was similar to that of going into Covent Garden, on a sunny summers day, and shouting "Anthrax" at the top of your voice. Anything attached hid and anything mobile made a rapid retreat to the nearest crevice. A large crayfish smiled rather self consciously, as a young and (hopefully) rather inexperienced fish made an extremely unwise choice of crevice, shooting out again rapidly, whistling the "Lone Ranger" theme tune, ruggedly, so that there should be no misinterpretation. Some fish panicked and swam into rock faces at high speed but the unconscious state they achieved must have been bliss compared to my state of embarrassment. I felt like a diabetes councillor at a chocolate's coming out party.

Eventually the torture ended and the sub-marine scene returned to normal. Anxious though I was to run away in case Albert attempted "16 going on 17" or one of the other well known melodies, I couldn't help but wonder how on earth a sea fan in a marine nature reserve gets to know Rogers and Hammerstein tunes.

So I asked.

This was a mistake.

The gist of the most unpleasant half-hour of my life was that some years previously an LP (Long Player, for those of you that remember vinyl), the "Sound of Music" soundtrack, had fallen off a rather posh yacht. Despite almost National Lottery like odds to the contrary this record had landed horizontally, with the hole in the middle perfectly placed on a small point of rock. When the tide rushed past the record revolved. It wasn't all that long before a large hermit crab, using a whelk shell as a weekend cottage, sat underneath the aforementioned piece of vinyl with the shell's pointy bit touching one of the tracks. Tidal streams did their stuff, whelk apex acted as a stylus, air space inside the shell acted like a sound box and Julie Andrews (at slightly the wrong speed) scared the snit out of every living marine being in the immediate vicinity.

Albert caught the first blast and every subsequent rendition tipped him gently into the abyss of insanity. The Sound of Music sound track, (at varying speeds and backwards fifty per cent of the time due to tidal indecision) is likely to send even the most stoic of individuals into mad bugger territory when played often enough. Before the hermit crab had got bored and moved away Albert had learnt the lot.

With not an awful lot better to do with his time Albert decided to put the story of the whole event to the music on the only side of the LP that he had heard. Then if any complete idiot asked him how he happened to know the "Maria" story he would sing his reply, loudly, out of tune and at the wrong speed for one half of a totally hideous half-hour.

I looked back on my recent near death experience with something like affection. A small ferret like creature, with a megaphone strapped to it's snout, being abused with a small birch twig would have made an infinitely more pleasing sound than Albert's racket.

It was definitely time to visit Ross.

The instructions for finding Ross were indelibly printed on my mind with the permanence that only nightmares can achieve. When I arrived it became obvious that Ross was not in the best of moods.

Swear words, curses and general invective were issuing forth from my next "contact" (secret agent term there) like balls from a particularly rabid tennis machine that had just been force fed an industrial strength sport's drink.

My expectations of what Ross would look like were vague but what I saw did not fit my hastily improvised identikit picture at all. Ross corals are difficult chaps to describe. If you imagine a hybrid produced as a result of questionable behaviour by a cauliflower, a punctured football and a naked brain you will be somewhere on the right track. This bizarre colonial organism, yes another one, was no longer in its prime. It may have started the day as an approximately round object but when I arrived there was a large box like structure occupying the space that had once been occupied by roundness.

It was rather a sad sight. Ross managed to give a description of the events leading up to his topological transformation but his delivery lacked punch. An ancient coal miner, boasting a lifelong involvement with Capstan full strength cigarettes, lying under a double decker bus packed with lead blocks would probably have made a better effort.

With lots of gasping and wheezing it became apparent that Ross, whilst enjoying a frenzied bout of filter feeding, had been crushed by a lobster pot. Being rather old and fragile, Ross did not respond well to this event. His survival as such was not threatened as these colonial chaps can cope with quite a bit of peripheral Armageddon but first prize in this years underwater equivalent of the Chelsea Flower Show now looked remote. Like a hermit bacterium on the Pleiades.

LOBSTER POT MEETS ROSS.

There was now a rather delicate diplomatic side to this unfortunate situation. I had to consider whether it was politic to ask Ross for directions to the LLF's hideout with a lobster pot placed firmly within hearing range. This might be rather like demanding to know the whereabouts of a Kurdish stronghold while giving Saddham Hussein a piggyback.

In the event any diplomatic musings where cut short as things took another lurch into weird city Arkansas. I heard the unmistakable sound of weeping and to my astonishment it was the lobster pot that was in need of a potkerchief.

For the next section of my, impressively unusual, limpety existence I listened in silent amazement as something that should have been as inanimate as an episode of Coronation Street told me it's life story. Apparently an awareness of existence existed when the pot was still in its constituent parts, a general background noise, cosmic radiation, type of thingy. When the pot was assembled a quantum leap in consciousness occurred but the initial, "Well what a smart, if rather perforated, box I am." turned to horror when the aforementioned recent convert to sentience realised what it was going to be used for.

Lobster pots were dreadfully upset when they were lowered on to the sea bed, smashing beautiful animals as they landed; they were ashamed and guilty when lobsters were attracted into their midst by cunningly placed bits of bait and they were mortified at the lobsters desperate attempts to escape and the subsequent fate that they met.

The pots never dared to talk to the lobsters as they believed the crustacean citizens must despise them deeply, so they just went on being miserable, hating their job even more than the people that have to appear on pet food adverts.

Well I was stunned. You could have put the whole of the electrical output of the nearest Nuclear (yes we are completely safe really, Chernobyl? oh that was just an isolated hiccup, honest guv) Power station straight through my private parts and I couldn't have been more frizzed. It was like meeting a vegetarian Tiger with a passion for Quiche Lorraine. Most unexpected.

If anything this meant making contact with the LLF was even more important than before but how was I going to get instructions in the present rather tricky diplomatic mine field?

Well "Pssssssssstt" was the thing that happened next. This was not the next thing I would have predicted but when "Pssssssssssstt" happened again it certainly got my attention. It has to be said that "Pssssssssssstt" was a more dynamic event than the lengthy period of indecision that I had pencilled in to my personal organiser.

"Pssssssssssssssstt" became an even more interesting alternative when a large stream of bubbles and a whispered "Over here Toss Brain." issued forth from a nearby dark crevice.

Naturally I slid over to investigate.

"If you want to meet the Lobster Liberation Front the next contact is the Jewel Anemone Supermodel Training Academy." (Otherwise known as JASTA, another one of these catchy little acronyms that just trip off the tongue.) "Follow the rock westwards 'til you get to a clump of dead men's sea fingers

(!), then go up onto the rock face, you can't miss the JASTA, they are all over the place."

"But what if the dead men's fingers are still attached to the dead man and he's not dead really but just pretending?" I asked rather nervously.

"Cretin" said the crevice "dead men's fingers is the name given to a type of colonial, white soft coral that grows in clumps and just looks like the fingers of dead men, but only if they have been in the water a long time."

"Oh fine" I replied, a little confused but also a little relieved. I felt I had had more than enough stress for one day without having to cope with close encounters with deceased sailors' body parts, let alone having to use them as route markers. The fact that the route markers only looked like a stiff's digits wasn't enough of a consolation to mollify my slightly ruffled non-existent molluscan feathers.

Off I went along the bottom of the rock face wondering firstly, if I was ever going to eat again and secondly, if I had really just held a conversation with a geographical feature. The food supply question was answered, at least in the short term, with a resounding "NO" as there was nothing remotely edible as far as the sensory apparatus could detect. This was followed by a resounding "BUGGER" as the digestive system got the message. The second question was still out with the jury when to my right I heard, "Sorry I called you toss brain, it was a bit rude." Immediately I was joined by a small fish who continued, " I thought I'd show you the way as I'm a bit bored."

Well I was delighted to have some company and pretty normal company at that. At least this new companion did not bombard me with Sound of Music favourites and it was rather comforting to be chatting with a chap that was definitely a chap and not a collection of chaplets joined together to form a colonial chap.

"I'm afraid I don't move very quickly, you might get bored," I said. "Don't worry," said my Piscine chum "I'll zig zag around a lot which is a pretty sound strategy for avoiding predators." So my new buddy zig zagged around and I slid. Pretty soon we came across a mass of four white, swollen fingery type projections, which I assumed must be the dead man's fingers.

As we approached the white mass, which to my complete non-surprise proved to be yet another colonial gathering, it started shouting "Wig, Wig, Wig", in a very high pitched voice. It went on shouting "Wig" continuously until my scaly chum head butted the largest finger at high speed. This seemed to have the desired effect as the digital delinquents shut up.

"What do you mean wig?" I said.

"You are wearing one, cone features," retorted one of the chaplets rather rudely.

" I most certainly am not." I replied, "What you are mistaking for a wig is actually a collection of bits of green seaweed growing on the top of my shell. I would be more than delighted to remove t all and stuff it hook, line and sinker into my extremely empty digestive system but that would involve leaving my shell and I don't like to do that in front of strangers."

My fishy friend looked rather put out at the mention of hooks and lines, which was tactless of me I suppose, but before a word of reproach got to leave the nursery the digital delinquents said.

"No it isn't, it's a wig. Whenever we see a wig it's our duty to shout "Wig" very loudly until the wig police arrive. Then the wig in question is escorted into custody for wigorous questioning until it tells the wig police what they need to know."

Well I spent a good 0.21 of a nanosecond wondering what on earth the "Wig Police" could possibly **need** to know when there was another uproar of "Wig,Wig,Wig." Even the fishes' best efforts couldn't quell the riot this time so we did the next best thing, we ran away.

While we ran (as in slithered and zig zagged) I caught myself worrying about what I would say to the wig police, if they ever caught up with us. Then I caught myself telling myself not to be so bloody stupid as there was no such thing as the wig police. Then I nervously enquired of my travelling companion if he thought there might really be a wig police, to which he replied that if he'd been asked to give odds on a sea fan krowing fifty per cent of the Sound of Music, he'd probably have used the term 'astronomical" in his reply, therefore since he was wrong anything was now a distinct possibility and we'd better run like hell. So we did.

Eventually our sliding and zig zagging brought us up to a fairly steep bit of rock where we were greeted by an astonishingly beautiful sight. The top of the rock graded into the roof of an underwater cave and all over its surface were hundreds of brightly coloured jewel anemones. Greens, golds, whites, pinks, oranges (the colour, not the fruit of course), browns, yellows and chimpanzees. (Sorry that was rather a pathetic attempt to see if you were still concentrating. I realise that I'm probably chancing my arm a bit giving you a test when you are being kind enough to read this in the first place, but there again what can you do? Put me in Paella probably).

Anyway it was a bit of a chromatic orgy, a visual cornucopia, a tantric gateway to eye ball nirvana AND hopefully my last way point en route to meeting the ever elusive LLF.

As we got closer to the jewel anemones we saw a little sign saying "Jewel Anemone Supermodel Training Academy- no uglies allowed." This I thought was not too good a sign, if you'll excuse the pun. Our worst fears were realised as we got closer to the Naomi Cambells of the deep; we heard the unmistakable sounds of bickering. This rather detracted from the aesthetic pant expander we had enjoyed earlier.

"You stole my heated tentacle rollers Aphrodite."

"Only because you nicked most of my setting gel Persephone."

"I did not Aphrodite, anyway you are looking like a lobsters backside today."

"Oh yes? Well for your information Persephone, you look just like you did yesterday and yesterday you looked like a mound of seal blubber."

"Well you're only jealous, bum features. That so called boyfriend of yours smells like a dead turtle and I've heard he wouldn't know longitudinal fission if it came and bit a tentacle off him."

Well conceivably Aphrodite's reply to this would have been unprintably rude but I never got to hear it because two other jewel anemones, Nigel and Jason, started hitting each other with dismembered crab's limbs, which made quite a racket.

Apparently the dispute this time was over the ownership of rather a beautiful, coloured contact lens that had floated into the cave and had been the source of considerable jealousy and rage ever since.

Just as my fishy chum and I were about to retreat, having given up all hope of making ourselves heard over the cacophony of anemone altercations, a loud, very authoritative voice bellowed "If you don't all shut up this instant you will be expelled from the Academy in disgrace and nobody will graduate."

Silence reigned.

"As punishment for this disgraceful behaviour in front of visitors the use of mirrors will be banned for 48 hours, starting immediately."

Silence settled itself in to the throne and looked quietly confident about breaking Queen Victoria's record as a reigning monarch. The mirror ban, apparently, was a terrible retribution in a community where Narcissus would have been ticked off for not paying enough attention to his own appearance. Tears were shed, tentacles wilted and for the only time in my life I saw the roof of a cave sulk as little mother of pearl mirrors were hidden away in secret cnidarian recesses.

The owner of the voice from Crowd Control Central happened to be an old, fairly large devonshire cup coral, no lightweight in the aesthetic stakes itself. Devonshire cup corals are similar to jewel anemones but they have a hard calcium carbonate bit in the middle which for mysterious pH related reasons makes them far less vain. As a result they often got jobs as supervisors in the Academy. They are more than capable of ruling with a rod of iron when things get a bit out of tentacle.

Quite obviously this was the woman we needed to speak to so we sidled over and outlined our mission. We discovered that her name was Devina and we got a rather long, lobster-potted (ho-ho) history of her life so far. This was far too tedious to even contemplate boring you with here but suffice it to say that "heated rollers" came into the plot a number of times as did "Wash and Bugger Off shampoo."

LARRY AND CHUM MEET ANGRY

J.A.S.T.A.

Unfortunately we also got an unsolicited resume of the history of the Academy. To my astonishment the early days of the JASTA movement stemmed from that good old Sound of Music record. A group of jewel anemones heard the sound track frequently while Ross was being tipped into the mentally disturbed abyss. During the chorus of "My favourite things," they thought they heard a reference to anemone stings. (Secretly I knew that it was "Bees" but thought silence was the best ploy in the circumstances.) The surprise discovery that anemones featured in a famous musical meant that an Academy had to be set up, immediately, to train potential Julie Andrews and Christopher Plummer anemones for when the inevitable underwater version of the musical was attempted.

At the time of writing hoards of Hollywood directors were conspicuous by their absence in and around the Skomer MNR but with the popularity of the film "Titanic," well anything's possible. The generally stressed and overwrought state of the Academy's occupants was a direct result of waiting for the appearance of "the Directors" for the whole of their short and fairly uneventful lives. If the Directors had turned up when the mirrors had been off limits for a couple of hours, the panic that would have ensued would have made Titanic's most fraught scenes seem like a disco for the recently dead.

Even for a broad minded limpet like myself things were beginning to get rather too surreal, so after what I hoped was a polite, "Gosh how interesting," I asked the million dollar question. Could Devina direct us to the LLF's hideout?

"Yes" she said. At this point there was one of those bizarre conversational gaps where nobody is quite sure whose go it is next. My Piscine chum and I waited for the gory details, grid references and time schedules to be emitted from Devina's persona, but nothing happened.

I began to wonder if a bribe was called for. I had seen an empty topshell shell on the way to the Academy, enough to make mother of pearl mirrors for the whole lot of them, and was just about to mention the fact when Devina spoke again.

"If you go down to the bottom of the rocks and head west you will come to a place called 'The Lantern,' it's a cave that goes right through to the other side of the Island. The LLF have their hideout on the left-hand side as you go in. We have another little part of the Academy stationed there so we got to know about the terrorists' existence fairly early on. We were sworn to secrecy at claw point but your mission sounds crisp, clean, wholesome and generally in tune with the American way so I'll wish you the best of luck. Now I must get back to my students as we have an intensive session on tentacle manicure planned for this afternoon and given the 'mirror situation,' there will be a riot if I'm late."

Now this was exciting stuff. No more go betweens, no more bowel wrenchingly awful renditions of the Sound of Music. I said a rather tearful farewell to my osteichthyean oppo, as he had fishy things to attend to and set out on the last part of my quest.

Climbing over mountains, snowfields and glacial moraine. Forging wild rapids. Dangling from lengths of creeper and drinking waterfalls dry. In total I had accomplished absolutely none of these heroic feats on my way to the LLF's hideout but it felt as if I had done the bloody lot by the time I espied my first eco-terrorist.

I suppose I was expecting lobsters with sub-machine guns or at least the odd Uzi 9mm. I had hoped for leather bullet belts around their carapaces, eye patches (optional) and maybe the odd towel around the head. A smattering of Semtex would have been nice, the odd tank and of course some smoulderingly rampant bits of lobster tot, scantily clad with more lipstick than you could shake a stick at.

Expectations were of course shattered (as in Ming vase meets Sammy the Steamroller) when I saw four rather meek, bespectacled individuals clustered

around a typewriter. They would have been slightly more ferocious looking if they had had a letter opener (a nice steel one) between them but the most dangerous piece of equipment that I could see was a very sharp pencil.

It was VERY sharp though.

I had rather expected to find large numbers of individuals smashing bricks with one jointed limb, whilst disembowelling life sized dummies of lobster-pot fishermen with a rusty knife, but no, (Ming vase stupid enough to come out for round two) these crustaceans of steel appeared to be composing a letter.

So engrossed were they in this government disabling subterfuge that I was able to sneak round and have a quick peep at the letter before the chaps even knew I was there.

The gist of the missive was as follows................

Dear Lobster-pot Fishermen,

Why do you continue to kill crabs and lobsters in a Marine Nature Reserve, which is meant to protect the animals and plants inside it?

Why do your lobster pots destroy sea fans, ross corals and other fragile marine species in a Reserve set up to protect them?

Why do you continue to overfish so that there are so few of us left?

Yourts concernedly,

The last few remaining Lobsters.

"Well why indeed?" I was forced to ejaculate.

Unfortunately my ejaculation was out loud so the four lobsters, that were desperately searching for some tippex so that they could get rid of the unwanted 'T' in yourts, were nearly shocked out of their body armour.

"Who the hell are you and how did you get here?" was their rather rude conversational starter. One of them reached for the VERY sharp pencil. I explained, somewhat hastily, about dropping from the sky and all the various little adventures that had occurred in the interim and they seemed to calm down. Then I played my ace by asking them if they knew that lobster pots hated being lobster pots? As I suspected they hadn't got a clue about this aspect of lobster pot psychology and it seemed to cause a great deal of excitement and claw waving.

"You mean there is potential for the LLF and the pots to join forces to smash the capitalist fishermen scum from the face of the political map?" said the youngest of the four. He said it with such revolutionary zeal that he made a supremely and brainspankingly stupid idea seem almost plausible. However the other seasoned campaigners wasted no time in pointing out the Jumbo jet sized holes in his plan and then proceeded to tell him where he could stick his political commie-pinko rhetoric. It would have involved at least two toothpicks and a very small hammer.

"That seems to be about the long and the short of it." I said hopefully. "Why don't I help you to arrange a meeting?"

"Would you really?" they said.

"Absolutely" I said. "I know just the very pot."

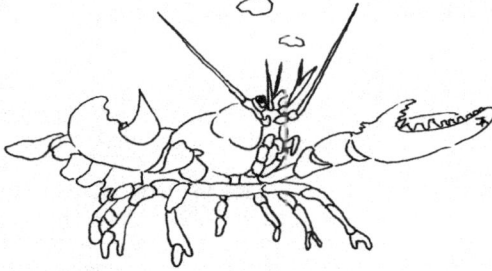

YOU MEAN THERE iS POTENTIAL FOR THE LLF AND THE POTS TO JOIN FORCES TO SMASH THE CAPITALIST FISHERMEN SCUM FROM THE FACE OF THE POLITICAL MAP?

A POLITICAL PEA BRAIN

GETS iT HORRIBLY WRONG.

So I did. And they did. There were lots of tears and recriminations. The pots put their side of the story about how they hated being lobster pots, how there didn't seem to be anything they could do about it and how they thought the lobsters must hate them deeply.

The lobsters explained that they had no idea that communication with lobster pots was possible, let alone desirable, but that this meeting had changed everything.

After all the tearful stuff was over the two parties got down to the serious business of discussing possible ways to sabotage future potting operations. The lobster pots explained how they had weak bits that were held together by string and that they wouldn't mind if the lobsters used their sharp claws to saw through them to escape. They would pass the word around the pot-vine so that all the pots could tell the lobsters which bits to cut.

Well it all ended in an extremely positive way and I felt a little thrill of pleasure knowing that I had helped to bring it all about. I had just decided that it was high time to exit stage left and was sidling off in that general direction when one of the LLF chaps spotted me.

There followed a hideously embarrassing "thank-you" ceremony in which I went as pink as an adolescent beetroot who had been caught pea molesting. Eventually I was allowed to escape without most of the ridiculously inappropriate presents that I had been offered, (limpets simply don't need state of the art food processors) and I boldly went.

It wasn't long before I remembered that I didn't have the remotest idea where I was going. Mission number one was successfully completed but that left a rather cold, outer reaches of space, type vacuum in the forward planner.

Time to stop and cogitate for a while.

I suppose that what happened when a disembodied voice said, "That's not quite the whole story." could be described as 'Cogitatus interruptus.'

Remembering that my last encounter with an unknown conversant had turned out rather favourably I stifled the "Sod the whole story, I'm hungry and I want to go home." rejoinder that had sprung to mind and contented myself with a polite, "Really? Do tell me more." Meanwhile I did rather a graceful 360° turn, which I had been practising at home for years without having a clue why, and spotted rather a large bull seal. It was hovering, about a foot above me, like a blubbery hovering thing.

Anyone who has had nightmares about being landed upon by a World War One Zeppelin will sympathise when I say that a pang of anxiety invaded my molluscan soft parts. Incidentally anyone who has had these nightmares might like to consider a long and expensive course of psychotherapy with the major part being centred around sexual rehabilitation.

Just a suggestion.

Well anyway the furry Zeppelin seemed benign enough, he immediately began to tell me about some of the other problems that existed within the Marine Reserve. To make the impact of the story a little more powerful my newly found adipose ridden buddy suggested that I slide on board and he would ferry me around to the very sites he was referring to.

We shot off North and then Westwards, out of the Lantern and along the North coast, past lots of lobster pots. I felt rather proud as I thought of the new situation there but then had a quick anxiety attack as it occurred to me that the lobster pot fishermen might change the design of the pots. If they used more plastic, instead of wood and string, the lobster pots might lose the ability to speak, they might even become inanimate.

Oh no.

I was just about to insist that the blubbery one put the brakes on and head back to the Lantern, quick, when he announced that we had arrived at a spot called the Garland Stone. Here he wished to tell me about fishing nets.

I could see why. Ahead of us was a pretty depressing sight. If Julius Caesar had come home from conquering the world to discover that Rome had been turned into a rehabilitation centre for gladiatorially challenged Christian vegetarians, he couldn't have been more upset.

A large curtain of virtually invisible netting had got caught on some rocks in front of us. The fact that the net had come adrift from its moorings and therefore was no longer a bona fide piece of fishing apparatus didn't seem to matter to the net one jot. It was still fishing away like Captain Birdseye on steroids and it had caught a phenomenal amount of stuff.

Fish in their hundreds were struggling unsuccessfully to get untangled. Even more depressing was the sight of a seal that had got caught up in the net and had drowned. My blubbery buddy looked extremely sad as he described how he had come upon nets like these that had killed dolphins and porpoises. On one occasion he even witnessed a human being get her diving gear caught in the net. It soon dawned on the diver that if she couldn't free herself pretty soon she was going to run out of air. Unless she had some pretty cunning anaerobic respiration party tricks to play she was going to be seriously stuffed in the making it back home for Christmas stakes. Luckily her diving buddy managed to free her and the integrity of Santa Clause's shopping list was preserved.

Seals, dolphins and porpoises don't generally carry diving knives around with them so if they get caught in the nets it's a different kettle of fish. Aaaaagh, bad choice of expression there, sorry.

Well I was feeling even more upset now. I did consider trying to cheer myself up with a rousing chorus of "My favourite things" but luckily I pulled myself back from the brink. Instead I settled for rather an insipid, "But I thought that this was a Marine Nature Reserve."

The seal replied, "You're quite right old boy. Apparently they have cocked up on the rules, even though it's a Marine Reserve certain people are allowed to come in to the protected area and kill things."

"That's a bit stupid isn't it?" I whined.

"Quite." he replied. "They are a funny bunch really. One lot set up these places to protect things, then another lot come in to the place and kill things and the first lot seem to have to let them do it."

"How odd." I ejaculated. Indeed if the aforementioned Julius Caesar's second discovery on coming home was that the Collosseum had been turned into a potty, for giants from the planet Anusol, he could hardly have understated the case more effectively.

"I'm afraid there is more." Said my hairy taxi. "Come and have a look at another part of the madness."

So I did.

We zonked around, at an astonishing speed for a chap used to unipodal slithering, and in two shakes of a buffalo gnats todger we arrived at a place called Wooltack Point.

It's on the mainland, facing Skomer, but it's still in the Marine Reserve. As we approached our next viewpoint I could see an unbelievable pile of junk on the seabed. Drink cans and glass bottles were obvious candidates for the most popular litter item of the year award but more alarming than this was the ridiculous amount of fishing line and lead weights.

The arrangement of fishing line and lead weights had a certain poetry to it. It was as if a diminutive superman had tied the line to his waist and had proceeded to play tag with every subatomic particle in the vicinity. The tangle was astonishing.

Unfortunately that was not the whole story. Many animals and plants were tangled up in this angler's junkyard. One sea fan, probably more than fifty years old judging by the size, was virtually cut off at the base by a bit of line. The next good tug from a decent bit of tidal current would have detached the poor old bugger from its mooring and rocketed it towards the North Wales coast like a flatulent banana from a missile launcher.

The chances of an unattached sea fan surviving are about as good as those of a Sicilian wearing a sandwich board reading "The Godfather's a dishonest, murdering, drug peddling tosser."

Not great.

"Where did all this garbage come from?" I asked in a suitably indignant tone of voice.

"Good question." the furry transportation device said to me. "Apparently there large numbers of human beings that derive tremendous pleasure from sitting, (or standing, let's not be positionist about this) dangling a line into the water with a hook on the end of it. The whole lot is suspended from a rod of some kind and the line is weighted so that it sinks."

"What's so exciting about that?" I enquired in slightly too high a voice, hurriedly adjusting the 'about that' portion of the question to a deep, bass growl.

"Ah well, the exciting bit is when you get to watch a fish die." Said the hirsute vehicle.

"But how do these two apparently unrelated activities connect?" said I. "How is the spatio-temporal coincidence of the two aforementioned apparently acausally related, thus synchronistic, phenomena achieved?" said I again, secretly worried that over exposure to the "Sound of Music" at the wrong speed, followed by the horrors of death and destruction in the Marine Reserve, had secretly tipped the balance of my molluscan mind.

The seal did look rather puzzled but then continued, "Well, these angling bods use the hook on the end of the line that I mentioned earlier. They place a tempting morsel on the hook for the fish to eat. Anything tasty, like bits of worm will do or even bits of shellfish. Then the fish comes along and thinks, "Ha ha, breakfast (or whatever meal is appropriate) eats the morsel, gets a hook through it's chops and is dragged out of Gaia's life sustaining fluids (vis. The sea) to suffocate, while anglers start thinking about chips."

"I see." I replied reflecting nervously on the appropriateness of limpet bodily tissue as a potential bait item. "And again, this happens in the Marine Reserve?"

"Absolutely." Replied my anti-glabrous Chevrolet. "It's refreshingly bonkers isn't it? No wonder the fish around here are scared shitless of human divers. Did you know that in some Marine Reserves in New Zealand there is a completely mind boggling concept?"

"Tell me more." I oozed co-operatively.

"Well in those Reserves nobody is allowed to do anything to harm the animals and plants."

"Get away." I exclaimed, hoping that this wasn't going to turn into a Travel Agent's commercial as I would then be rather buggered on the transport front. Meanwhile I wondered how the hell a limpet is supposed to know what is going on in New Zealand nature reserves. I then went on to wonder how the hell a seal gets to know. Good manners prevailed though and I refrained from asking my follicle ridden bicycle if he was drinking his own bath water. Just as well really as the next communication from my body-bearded buddy revealed all.

"Yes, some barnacles from that region arrived in British waters many years ago and because it's really one ocean, between us and the antipodes, they still manage to keep in contact with the chums back home. They told me that the fish in these New Zealand reserves all go bonkers when a diver arrives as divers feed fish. This time the fish don't get to die for the privilege of receiving a tasty morsel. The divers are happy because they get to see lots of pretty fish and the fish get happy because their stomachs are filled. It's a rather neat arrangement really."

"Don't the fishermen object?" I demanded, feeling a sudden and totally inexplicable affinity for the ravagers of the deep.

"They did at first." Replied my anti-Immac associate. "But then it dawned on them that the fish in the reserve would breed like happy breeding things, thereby producing more fish than the reserve could support. The extra fish would try to make a living in the world outside the reserve thus providing a good catch for the fishermen."

"So the fishermen actually like the reserve now?" I said, amazed at the, it's obvious when you think about it really, quality of the whole thing.

"Correct." Replied my razor-less mini-bus.

"Well why the hell doesn't it work like that over here?" I said in an exasperated molluscan fashion.

"I have thought about that one a lot, my calcium carbonate covered little amigo. The only conclusion that I can come too is..........................."

"Yes?"

"That they are a bunch of short sighted morons."

"Yes," I replied "It's pretty obvious when you look at it that way."

2. Larry goes home on purpose.

Having entertained ourselves with marine conservational banter for a while my furry buddy and I started to get a little restless. It seemed that the Skomer Marine Reserve was a jolly good thing. It also seemed that it would be a lot better if some of the rules were changed, well in fact all the rules were changed to just one. **"Nobody is allowed to do anything to harm the animals and plants."** Simple really and it makes for very short rulebooks.

Well having put the Marine Reserve's issues into the coffee percolator and observed them coming out a reassuring brown colour, my thoughts drifted, once again, in a distinctly homeward direction.

I was hungry, as in my digestive apparatus thought I was either dead or had gone bonkers and was attempting a photosynthetic lifestyle without a single bit of chlorophyll in the equation.

I was homesick, even though my home probably approximated to a highland games breakfast party, for particularly clumsy participants, where somebody had left the porridge at home and had brought along some crude oil instead.

I was keen to get home to see if any of my chums were around. I might even be able to muster up a slightly relieved sigh if not quite all the dogwhelks had died. The sigh would probably have to be amplified up to stadium blasting proportions, by a timpanically challenged Bon Jovi sound technician, to be heard, but it would be there, sort of.

And what of chitons? What indeed. Would they forgive me for the little hiccup on the recall front in "Larry and His Pals?"

All these unknowns. If I had had any hair, I would have been pulling it out by the wheelbarrow full with worry. If I had had nails, you could have crazy paved most of Alpha Centauri with the bitten off bits. Incidentally you could also have populated this, recently paved, celestial body with cunningly crafted artificial woolly mammoths, made from the wheelbarrows full of hair I would have pulled out if I had had any. Yes, I was that worried.

Luckily my hirsute sausage shaped chum was itching to visit some particularly reliable and juicy fishing grounds, conveniently near my erstwhile home. When the opportunity of a lift presented itself, it (the opportunity) was stuffed in armour and knighted before anybody could say, "Did anyone remember the tin opener?"

Off we went. Luckily the tide was in our favour the whole way so we completed the trip rather rapidly. A cork emerging from a champagne bottle that had pogoed the night away at a punk revival party would have been extremely hard pushed to have beaten me to it.

My bearded torpedo-like pal got me home in a jiffy. Not content with that, he obligingly swam along the shore, with me sitting on his head like a ridiculously small Chinese hat, until I was able to locate my home scar. Mercifully it was still unoccupied.

LARRY AND CHUM LOCATE HOME SCAR.

I trundled up the rocks, which were reassuringly familiar, and settled down chez moi. The shell, which had had minimal maintenance (400 metre service sort of thing) while I had been away, had to be fine tuned to the contours of the rock but soon I was clamped to the surface like, well like a limpet really. The seal my shell made with the rocks was so good that it would have foiled the attempts of even the most adept member of the subatomic limbo dancing society to get underneath it.

Having attended to territorial basics, food was definitely the next priority, much like revenge would be if you had just spent your summer holiday up to the neck in sand, while young children flicked your nose with small, extremely flexible sticks.

Well, good grief, the place was heaving with it (food that is). You may remember that I like nothing more than a damnedly good ten rounds with the green stuff that looks a lot like floppy grass. In terms of food availability, it was like a Sainsbury's store geared up for the festive season, BUT at this particular branch they were expecting the whole population of China AND the

Chinese had been informed that it was a matter of national pride that they out ate the Americans.

In short the place was green. The reason for the green nature of my home was quite simple, a lot of the chaps that eat green stuff, namely limpets, topshells and periwinkles et al., were dead, as in killed by the oil.

A casual look at the shore would confirm the havoc that had been wreaked amongst my herbivorous chums. Empty shells were lying around in their hundreds (as you would expect them to be really, empty shells are not renowned for their tap dancing abilities) Many of the barnacle's bungalows were full of air but decidedly empty of barnacle. Barnacles are not the sort of coves that pop round to the corner shop for a pint of milk, returning later to the bosom of their loved ones. If they are out, then they are really out, as in dead, stiff, moribund, tickling the tharatoid toadstool's testicles with an extremely short handled feather duster.

Still the news was not all bad. There were also a lot fewer dogwhelks and crabs. One doesn't like to make merry at the expense of other inter-tidal denizens but on this occasion I was prepared to make an exception.

After a fairly rapid assessment of the Sea Empress legacy I decided to get firmly stuck into my first meal. The one big advantage of being a survivor on a recovering seashore is that you aren't going to starve. As I rasped (technical term for chomped) I considered my new situation. Plenty of room, plenty of food, fewer predators. God I even began to feel positively grateful to the Sea Empress. Then I realised what a totally ludicrous line of thought that was and put it all down to post travel shock. Being grateful for a few tender mercies after a large oil spill is a bit like being grateful for a brand new pair of (top of the range) designer sunglasses which arrived after being delayed in the post, minutes after one's head had been cut off. A mite too positive I feel. I'm as committed to positive thinking as the next archaeogastropod but there are limits.

Temporal Interlude approximating to twelve lunar cycles.

Hello there.

Cock up on the continuity front I'm afraid. All the excitement of arriving home quite put the writing of memoirs out of one's head. Time has passed. (Just as well really, time with constipation would cause some pretty hideous problems, physically and philosophically.)

I think it must be about a year.

The shore has shown some reassuring signs of recovery though it will be a couple of years before things settle down properly. Some chaps have suffered more than others. Rumours have circulated about a population of rather rare starfish across the bay, that were nearly wiped out by the oil. They don't have young that float in the sea so there is no chance of the cavalry arriving by Zodiac. They had better do some pretty frenzied reproducing, that would be my advice. Hopefully they won't suffer the horrors of inbreeding and produce a mutant starfish that is a gifted quantum physicist. Now that would be a serious waste of genetic material.

There was a cat once that was good at quantum physics but I think it got killed, or did it? Ho ho, in-joke there for any of Schrodinger's mates that might be reading this, I'm sure there must be flocks of them. (Flocks? I wonder what the collective noun for a group of quantum physicists is. A quark? A superposition? An uncertainty? Who knows? Yes there we have it folks, a rib tickler for the Heisenberg fraternity.)

Now where was I? (Hee hee, further mirth for the uncertainty brigade.)

Ahhh yes. The shore recovering: good news. Some things have changed in a rather more permanent way however. Tricky business finding the right words to explain. I have told you some fairly embarrassing stuff about limpets previously. I was able to say it in a fairly rugged, "Isn't it about time to paint the tank again?" sort of way.

You may remember the little detail about us, or at least some of us, changing sex? I expect you were reassured by the fact that the author of the missive that you were reading at the time hadn't changed sex. I know I would be.

Hmmmmm. Well the shore went on recovering and I went on being a limpet, a male limpet, hence the name. I got bigger but luckily I still had plenty of room around the home scar thanks to the Sea Empress. Aaaaaaagh, there you see? I'm doing it again; I put "Thanks" and "Sea Empress" in to the same sentence. Good grief.

I remember the day rather well; it was towards the beginning of autumn. Sea temperatures were falling and the water began to get rough in a "This is for real, no more mister nice guy." sort of way. And I just thought it. No preamble. Straight out with it, as fluently as any other thought that I had ever had.

"I hope the eggs are OK"

Followed by.

"Whaaaaat!" "Eggs?" "Girls have eggs, chaps have swimmy things."

Followed by.

"Oh my God, I'm a girl."

Followed by.

"Oh my God, I'm a girl."

Followed by.

"Eeeeek, Aargg."

So there we have it. You have just ploughed your way through the second volume of the memoirs of a limpet called Larry. Some of you with stainless steel constitutions may even have ploughed your way through volume one of the same. (If you didn't end up gibbering in a corner you have my profound respect.) You are convinced that Larry, the hero, is wholesome, rugged, clean, crisp and above reproach. Up to a few months ago you were right.

Now how about if I roll this past you and see if it hits the back of the net?

I'm still wholesome, rugged(ish), clean, crisp and above reproach but in a slightly more girlie way. And finally,

from now on, ... I WISH TO BE CALLED

LAURA.

THE END (almost certainly.)

www.ingramcontent.com/pod-product-compliance
Lightning Source LLC
Chambersburg PA
CBHW032107080426
42733CB00006B/451